Sounds Like
American

A Guide to Fluency in Spoken English

Ann Cook

Atsushi Mishima

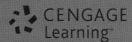

Sounds Like American [Text Only]—A Guide to Fluency in Spoken English

Written by Ann Cook and adapted by Atsushi Mishima

© 2010 Cengage Learning K.K.

Original edition © 2000 Ann Cook. *American Accent Training, 2nd Edition* by Ann Cook.
ISBN: 978-0-7641-7369-1.

For permission to use material from this textbook or product, **e-mail to eltjapan@cengage.com**

ISBN: 978-4-86312-418-9

Cengage Learning K.K.
No 2 Funato Building 5th Floor
1-11-11 Kudankita, Chiyoda-ku
Tokyo 102-0073
Japan

Tel: 03-3511-4392
Fax: 03-3511-4391

はじめに

「ジャイーチェッ」

　これはあるアメリカ人が発音したことばを、日本人にどう聞こえたかカタカナで書き取ってもらったものですが、どういう意味だか分かりますか。もちろん英語です。中学生でも知っていそうな文です。どうでしょう。

　正解は Did you eat, yet? です。なぜ「ディッド・ユー・イート・イェット」ではなく、「ジャイーチェッ」に聞こえたのでしょう。Did は [dɪd]（ディッド）、you は [juː]（ユー）、eat は [iːt]（イート）、yet は [jet]（イェット）という発音なので、これを並べて文にすれば発音は当然 [dɪdjuːiːtjet]（ディッドユーイートイェット）になるはずです。日本語なら、「あなた」「もう」「食べた」を順番に１つずつ発音しても、「あなたもう食べた？」と一息で言っても、個々の音の発音はほとんど変わりません。しかし、残念ながら英語はそうはいかないのです。

　英語には日本語にはない音があり、そのような音を正しく発音できるようになるのは大切なことです。本書では日本人が苦手とする英語の母音や子音の練習もたくさん用意しています。ただ、いくら個別の音や単語が正確に発音できても、それだけでは英語らしい発音にはなりません。英語は日本語と違い、単語を１つ１つ読み上げたときと、文中に出てくるときとでは発音が大きく異なるからです。では、なぜ発音が変わるのか。その原因はアクセント、リズム、イントネーションと呼ばれる英語のプロソディーにあります。プロソディーは、ことばの全体的な印象や「らしさ」を生み出します。ネイティブスピーカーのように英語を発音するには、この英語のプロソディーをマスターしなければいけません。本書はアメリカ英語に的を絞り、まず英語のプロソディーを徹底的に練習します。英語と日本語のプロソディーはかなり違うため最初は戸惑うことも多いでしょう。しかし、練習を重ねていけば必ずマスターできます。あきらめずに根気よく練習を続けてください。Did you eat it, yet? が [dʒəiːtʃət]（ジャイーチェッ）になる「からくり」は本書を読み終わったころに分かるようになるはずです。それでは、がんばりましょう！

Contents

本書の発音記号は基本的に『ジーニアス英和大辞典』に従いました。
ただし、表記は厳密さよりも学習者の使い勝手を優先しています。

UNIT 1

ネイティブ発音への道

1　英語らしい発音とは

まず、英語らしく発音するコツを3つご紹介しましょう。

単語を1つ1つ区切って発音しない

たとえば Bob is on the phone. と言う場合、各単語の後にポーズを置き、Bob, is, on, the, phone のように発音した方が1つ1つの単語がはっきり聞こえ通じやすいように思えますが、実際はその逆です。頻繁にポーズを入れると英語のリズムが乱れ、かえって分かりにくくなります。

単語よりも大きな単位で発音すること

英語を話すときは、複数の単語からなる「音のグループ」を1つの単位として発音することを意識してください。Bob is on the phone. なら Bob と phone を強く、それ以外の単語は弱く素早く発音します。そして、強い単語とその後に続く弱い単語を1つのグループとして一気に発音するのです。**Bob is on the phone.** ではなく、**Bob**isonthe **phone**. のように発音した方がネイティブらしい発音になるのです。

メリハリをつけること

今も見たように、英語では文中のすべての単語が同じ強さで発音されるわけではありません。強く発音される単語もあれば弱く発音される単語もあります。ある単語を他の単語より強く発音することを、アクセントを置くと言います。アクセントの位置を間違えると、文の意味が変わってしまうこともあるので注意しましょう。

2　アクセントとは

「強く発音する」とは具体的にはどういうことなのでしょう。「強く」というと息をたくさん吐き出すイメージを持たれるかもしれませんが、実はそうではありません。英語のアクセントで一番大切なのは、**声の高さを大きく変えること（＝ピッチを大きく変化させること）**です。

低いピッチで話しているときに急に声を上げたり、逆に高いピッチで話しているときに急に声を下げたりすると、その部分は他よりも目立って聞こえます。これが英語の

アクセントの正体です。アクセントは普通、文の意味を伝える上で重要な語に置かれ、どの文も必ず 1 つはアクセントを受ける単語を含んでいます。また、アクセントを受ける部分は他の所よりも長くなります（Unit 2 を参照）。この点に注意しながらまずアクセントの練習をしてみましょう。

Exercise 1-1

音声の後について A 〜 D のリストを繰り返し読んでください。アクセントのある所は太字になっています。強く発音するときは、ピッチを大きく変化させること（ここでは他の所より声を上げること）、その音を長く発音することを忘れないようにしましょう。リストは、まず左から右に向かって、その後、上から下に向かって読まれています。

CD 1-2

A	B	C	D
1. **duh** duh **duh**	1. **la** la la	1. **mee** mee **mee**	1. **ho** ho ho
2. duh duh **duh**	2. la la **la**	2. mee mee **mee**	2. ho ho **ho**
3. duh **duh** duh	3. la **la** la	3. mee **mee** mee	3. ho **ho** ho
4. **duh** duh duh	4. **la** la la	4. **mee** mee mee	4. **ho** ho ho

A 〜 D を 1. 〜 4. の順番で読んでください。各列が同じアクセントパターンになるよう注意しましょう。

CD 1-3

A	B	C	D
1. **duh** duh **duh**	1. duh duh **duh**	1. duh **duh** duh	1. **duh** duh duh
2. A B **C**	2. impre**cise**	2. con**dition**	2. **al**phabet
3. 1 2 **3**	3. a hot **dog**	3. a **hot** dog	3. **hot** dog stand
4. **Dogs** eat **bones.**	4. They eat **bones.**	4. They **eat** them.	4. **Give** me one.

3 英語の基本的なアクセントパターン

① 名詞＋動詞＋名詞（Dogs eat bones.）

では、基本的な文のアクセントパターンを練習してみましょう。まずは、名詞＋動詞＋名詞からなる文です。英語は初めて話題に上る名詞（＝新情報）にアクセントを置くのが原則です。

Dogs | eat | bones.

音声の後について、2つの名詞にアクセントを置いて読んでください。同じような文を自分でも作って発音してみましょう。

1. **Dogs** eat **bones**.
2. **Mike** likes **bikes**.
3. **Elsa** wants a **book**.
4. **Adam** plays **pool**.
5. **Bobby** needs some **money**.
6. **Susie** combs her **hair**.
7. **John** lives in **France**.
8. **Nelly** teaches **French**.
9. **Ben** writes **articles**.
10. **Keys** open **locks**.
11. **Jerry** makes **music**.
12. **Jean** sells some **apples**.
13. **Carol** paints the **car**.
14. **Bill** and I fix the **bikes**.
15. Ann and **Ed** call the **kids**.
16. The **kids** like the **candy**.
17. The **girls** have a **choice**.
18. The **boys** need some **help**.
19. _____
20. _____

② 代名詞＋動詞＋代名詞　（They **eat** them.）

次は、代名詞＋動詞＋代名詞からなる文です。代名詞はすでに出てきた話題（＝旧情報）を指すことばで、強く発音しません。代わりに動詞がアクセントを受けます。

They | eat | them.

一般に名詞は新情報、代名詞は旧情報を表し、下記の2つの文が英語の基本的なアクセントパターンになります。

```
Dogs          bones.
        eat
They          them.
```

音声では左から右に向かって読まれています。左側の文では名詞に、右側の文では動詞にアクセントを置いて発音してください。自分でも同じような文を作って発音してみましょう。

1. **Bob** sees **Betty**.	He **sees** her.
2. **Betty** knows **Bob**.	She **knows** him.
3. Ann and **Ed** call the **kids**.	They **call** them.
4. **Jan** sells some **apples**.	She **sells** some.
5. **Jean** sells **cars**.	She **sells** them.
6. **Bill** and I fix the **bikes**.	We **fix** them.
7. **Carl** hears **Bob** and me.	He **hears** us.
8. **Dogs** eat **bones**.	They **eat** them.
9. The **girls** have a **choice**.	They **have** one.
10. The **kids** like the **candy**.	They **like** it.
11. The **boys** need some **help**.	They **need** something.
12. **Ellen** should call her **sister**.	She should **call** someone.
13. The **murderer** killed the **plumber**.	He **killed** a man.
14. The **tourists** went **shopping**.	They **bought** stuff.
15. _____	_____
16. _____	_____
17. _____	_____
18. _____	_____
19. _____	_____
20. _____	_____

アクセントが置かれる単語に下線を引き、実際に発音してみましょう。

1. Sam sees Bill.	7. You and Bill read the news.
2. She wants one.	8. It tells one.
3. Betty likes English.	9. Bernard works in the restaurant.
4. They play with them.	10. He works in one.
5. Children play with toys.	11. He sees him.
6. Bob and I call you and Bill.	12. Mary wants a car.

13. She likes it.

14. They eat some.

15. Len and Joe eat some pizza.

16. We call you.

17. You read it.

18. The news tells a story.

19. Mark lived in France.

20. He lived there.

4 アクセントの働き

アクセントは文の中でいろいろな役割を果たします。ここでは4つのケースを見てみましょう。アクセントを受けた単語は太字で書かれています。

① 新情報

It sounds like **rain**. （雨のようだ）

「3. 英語の基本的なアクセントパターン」でも見たように、英語では初めて話題に上る名詞にアクセントを置きます。

② 含意

It **sounds** like rain, but I don't think it **is**.
（雨音のように聞こえるが、雨だとは思わない）

sound にアクセントを置くことで、字面とは反対の意味を持たせることができます。
It **looks** like a diamond, but I think it's a **zircon**. （ダイヤモンドのように見えるが、ジルコンだと思う）、It **smells** like Chanel, but at that price, it's a **knock**-off. （シャネルのような香りだが、あの値段からすると、本物じゃないだろう）、It **feels** like . . . や It **tastes** like . . . なども同じパターンです。

It sounds like **rain**. （＝雨だろう）
It **sounds** like rain. （＝しかし、雨ではない）

③ 対比

He **likes** rain, but he **hates** snow.
（彼は雨は好きだが、雪は嫌いだ）

Is the book **on** the table or **under** it?
（その本はテーブルの上にあるのか、それとも下にあるのか）

「X は…だが、Y は…である」「X ではなく Y である」など2つの語を対比したいときは、対比させる両方の語にアクセントを置きます。

④ 否定

> It **can't rain** when there're no **clouds**.
> (雲もないのに雨であるわけがない)

助動詞は通常アクセントを受けませんが、-n't のついた否定形はアクセントを受けます。

音声の後について 1.〜4. の文を繰り返し発音してみましょう。それぞれの意味がうまく伝わるよう正しい位置にアクセントを置くことを忘れずに。

1. It sounds like **rain**.
2. It **sounds** like rain.
3. He **likes** rain, but he **hates** snow.
4. It **can't rain** on my **parade**! He **can't do** it.

吹き込まれている 1.〜4. の内容を伝えるには、Exercise 1-5 に出てきた 4 つの文のうちどれが一番適当でしょう。発信音の後すぐに声に出して言ってみてください。(リスニングが苦手な人は、下の英文を読んだ後、言ってみましょう)。

1. Convey the opinion that although it has the sound of rain, it may be something else.
2. Convey the fact that rain is an impossibility right now.
3. Convey the information that it really does sound as if rain is falling.
4. Convey the different feelings that someone has about rain and snow.

5 アクセントが生み出す意味

アクセントの位置を変えることで、文の意味を変えたり、微妙なニュアンスを出したりすることができます。

Exercise 1-7   CD 1-8

"pretty good" という語句は、pretty と good のどちらにアクセントを置くかによって、文の意味が変わります。音声の後について発音してみましょう。

Question: How did you like the movie?
  Answer: 1. It was pretty **good**. (= She liked it.)
           2. It was **pretty** good. (= She didn't like it much.)

Exercise 1-8   CD 1-9

同じ文でも、使われる場面や話し手の意図により、アクセントの位置は変わります。音声の後について発音してみましょう。

1. What would you **like**?
   (この文ではこのアクセントパターンが最も普通。単に相手に何が好きなのか、欲しいのか尋ねている)

2. What would **you** like?
   (何人かいる中で、「**あなたは**何が好きなのか、何が欲しいのか」と you を強調して尋ねるときのアクセントパターン)

3. What **would** you like?
   (相手の好みについていろいろと話した後、「具体的にどれにしたいのか、どれが欲しいのか」と尋ねたいときのアクセントパターン。たとえば、"Now that you mention it, what **would** you like?" など。または、相手がこちらの提案を立て続けに拒んだため、少しうんざりして、"If you don't want any of these, what **would** you like?" と言うときなど)

4. **What** would you like?
   (相手の言ったことがよく聞こえなかったので、「もう一度繰り返してほしい」と頼むときのアクセントパターン。または、「相手の言ったことが信じられない」と伝えたいとき。たとえば、"I'd like strawberry jam on my asparagus."—"**What** would you like?" など)

次もアクセントの位置を変えることで、文のニュアンスが変わる例です。音声の後について発音してみましょう。

1. **I** didn't say he stole the money. Someone **else** said it.
   （自分ではなく、他の誰かが言った）

2. I **didn't** say he stole the money. **That's** not true at **all**.
   （自分が言ったと思われているようだが、事実無根だ）

3. I didn't **say** he stole the money. I only **suggested** the **possibility**.
   （ほのめかしたことはあったかもしれないが、はっきりとは言わなかった）

4. I didn't say **he** stole the money. I think someone **else** took it.
   （彼が盗んだのではなく、他の人が盗んだ）

5. I didn't say he **stole** the money. Maybe he just **borrowed** it.
   （確かに彼は金を取ったが、盗んだのではなく、何か他の動機があるはずだ）

6. I didn't say he stole **the** money, but rather some **other** money.
   （彼は金を盗んだとは思うが、その金だとは思わない）

7. I didn't say he stole the **money**. He may have taken some **jewelry**.
   （確かに彼は盗みをしたが、盗んだのは金ではなく、他のものだ）

吹き込まれている 1.〜 7. の内容を伝えるには、Exercise 1-9 に出てきた 7 つの文のうちどれが一番適当でしょう。発信音の後すぐに声に出して言ってください。数秒後には正解文が読まれます。（リスニングが苦手な人は、下の英文を読んだ後、言ってみましょう）。

1. Indicate that he borrowed the money and didn't steal it.
2. Indicate that you are denying having said that he stole it.
3. Indicate that you think he stole something besides money.
4. Indicate that you were not the person to say it.
5. Indicate that you don't think that he was the person who stole it.
6. Indicate that you didn't say it outright, but did suggest it in some way.
7. Indicate that he may have stolen a different amount of money.

6 頭字語、スペリング、数字のアクセント

頭字語や単語のスペリング、数字を読み上げるときは、その最後の文字、数字にアクセントを置きます。音声の後について発音してみましょう。

頭字語	
IBM	IB**M**
MIT	MI**T**
Ph.D.	Ph.**D.**
MBA	MB**A**
LA	L**A**
IQ	I**Q**
RSVP	RSV**P**
TV	T**V**
USA	US**A**
ASAP	ASA**P**
CIA	CI**A**
FBI	FB**I**
USMC	USM**C**
COD	CO**D**
SOS	SO**S**
X, Y, Z	X, Y, **Z**

スペリング	
Box	B O **X**
Cook	C O O **K**
Wilson	W I **L**, S O **N**

数字	
Area Code	21**3**
Zip Code	9470**8**
Date	9/6/6**2**
Phone Number	55**5**-913**2**

7 文章を使った練習

では、最後にアクセントに注意して文章を読む練習です。音声の後について発音してみましょう。

Hello, **my** name is Ann. I'm taking American **Accent** Training. There's a **lot** to learn, but I **hope** to make it as **enjoyable** as possible. I should pick **up** on the American **intonation** pattern pretty **easily**, although the **only** way to **get** it is to **practice** all of the time. I use the **up** and down, or **peaks** and valleys, **intonation** more than I **used** to. I've been paying attention to **pitch**, **too**. It's like **walking** down a **stair**case. I've been **talking** to a lot of **Americans** lately, and they tell me that I'm **easier** to under**stand**. Anyway, I could go **on** and on, but the **important** thing is to **listen** well and sound **good**. **Well**, what do you **think**? **Do** I?

UNIT 2

英語のアクセントとリズム

1 単語のストレスとアクセント

英単語には他よりも目立って聞こえる音節が必ず1つあります。これをストレス音節と言います。ストレスを受ける音節は、他の音節よりも**高く、長く、丁寧**に発音されます。cat のような1音節語は単語全体がストレスを受けますが、2音節以上の語では単語ごとにストレスを受ける音節が決まっています。厳密な定義はともかく、音節は原則として母音を含むことから、母音にストレスを置くことを意識するとよいでしょう。ストレスの位置を間違えると意味が通じなくなったり、誤解されることもあるので注意が必要です。実際、machine を誤って **ma**chine と発音してしまうと、ネイティブスピーカーは、その間違ったストレスパターンに合う単語を無意識のうちに探そうとします。それくらいストレスの位置は重要なのです。Unit 1 で「アクセントを受ける単語」という言い方をしましたが、正確にはアクセントを受けるのは、その単語のストレス音節です。

Exercise 2-1　　　　　　　　　　　　　　　　　　　　　　　　　　　　CD 1-14

音声の後について、ストレスの位置に注意しながら繰り返してみましょう。太字になっているのがストレス音節です。

1 音節語				
jump	**box**	**cat**		
dog	**see**	**plan**		

2 音節語				
project	**sun**set	**icy**	**suit**case	
des**troy**	pre**tend**			

3 音節語				
analyze	**ar**ticle	**di**gital	**an**alog	**din**nertime
to**mor**row	what**ever**	po**ta**to		

4 音節語				
permanently	**de**monstrated	**ca**tegory	**ed**ucator	
ana**lys**is	in**vis**ible			
imi**ta**tion	ana**lyt**ic			

2 ストレスと品詞

英語にはストレスの位置が変わると品詞が変わってしまう単語がいくつかあります。
ここでまとめて練習しましょう。

Exercise 2-2 CD 1-15

以下の各ペアの単語は、第1音節から第2音節にストレスが移ると名詞から動詞に変わってし
まいます。音声の後について発音してみましょう。ストレスのあった音節からストレスが消え
ると、母音が変わることもあるので注意してください。

＊ 発音記号中のアポストロフィーは弱い母音のため音が消えてしまうことがあることを示しています。

名詞		動詞	
an **ac**cent	[æks'nt]	to ac**cent**	[æksent]
a **con**cert	[kɑnsəʳt]	to con**cert**	[k'nsəʳt]
a **con**flict	[kɑnflɪkt]	to con**flict**	[k'nflɪkt]
a **con**test	[kɑntest]	to con**test**	[k'ntest]
a **con**tract	[kɑntrækt]	to con**tract**	[k'ntrækt]
a **con**trast	[kɑntræst]	to con**trast**	[k'ntræst]
a **con**vert	[kɑnvəʳt]	to con**vert**	[k'nvəʳt]
a **con**vict	[kɑnvɪkt]	to con**vict**	[k'nvɪkt]
a **de**fault	[diːfɑːlt]	to de**fault**	[d'fɑːlt]
a **de**sert	[dezəʳt]	to de**sert**	[d'zəʳːt]
a **dis**charge	[dɪstʃɑəʳdʒ]	to dis**charge**	[d'stʃɑəʳdʒ]
an **en**velope	[env'loʊp]	to en**vel**op	[envel'p]
an **in**cline	[ɪnklaɪn]	to in**cline**	[ɪnklaɪn]
an **in**sert	[ɪnsəʳt]	to in**sert**	[ɪnsəʳːt]
an **in**sult	[ɪns'lt]	to in**sult**	[ɪnsʌlt]
an **ob**ject	[ɑbdʒekt]	to ob**ject**	[əbdʒekt]
perfect	[pəʳːf'kt]	to per**fect**	[pəʳfekt]
a **per**mit	[pəʳːmɪt]	to per**mit**	[pəʳmɪt]
a **pre**sent	[prez'nt]	to pre**sent**	[pr'zent]
produce	[proʊdjuːs]	to pro**duce**	[pr'djuːs]
progress	[prɑgr's]	to pro**gress**	[pr'gres]
a **pro**ject	[prɑdʒekt]	to pro**ject**	[pr'dʒekt]
a **pro**noun	[proʊnaʊn]	to pro**nounce**	[pr'naʊns]
a **pro**test	[proʊtest]	to pro**test**	[pr'test]

名詞		動詞	
a **re**bel	[**rebl**]	to re**bel**	[r'**bel**]
a **re**call	[**ri:kɑ:l**]	to re**call**	[r'**kɑ:l**]
a **re**cord	[**rekəʳd**]	to re**cord**	[r'**kɔəʳd**]
a **re**ject	[**ri:dʒekt**]	to re**ject**	[r'**dʒekt**]
research	[**ri:səʳ:tʃ**]	to re**search**	[r'**səʳ:tʃ**]
a **sub**ject	[**sʌbdʒekt**]	to sub**ject**	[s'**bdʒekt**]
a **sur**vey	[**səʳ:veɪ**]	to sur**vey**	[səʳ**veɪ**]
a **sus**pect	[**sʌs**pekt]	to sus**pect**	[s's**pekt**]

次の各ペアの単語は、ストレスの位置は変わりませんが、名詞や形容詞のとき語尾の -ate は弱く [ət] と発音されるのに対し、動詞になるときはそのまま [eɪt] と発音されます。音声の後について練習してみましょう。

名詞／形容詞		動詞	
advocate	[**ædv**'kət]	to **ad**vocate	[**ædv**'keɪt]
animate	[**æn**'mət]	to **an**imate	[**æn**'meɪt]
alternate	[**ɑ:ltəʳ**nət]	to **al**ternate	[**ɑ:ltəʳ**neɪt]
ap**pro**priate	[ə**proʊ**priət]	to ap**pro**priate	[ə**proʊ**prieɪt]
ap**prox**imate	[ə**præks**ɪmət]	to ap**prox**imate	[ə**præks**ɪmeɪt]
ar**tic**ulate	[ɑəʳ**tɪkj**ələt]	to ar**tic**ulate	[ɑəʳ**tɪkj**əleɪt]
as**so**ciate	[ə**soʊʃ**iət]	to as**so**ciate	[ə**soʊʃ**ieɪt]
de**lib**erate	[d'**lɪb**'rət]	to de**lib**erate	[d'**lɪbəʳ**eɪt]
dis**crim**inate	[d'**skrɪm**'nət]	to dis**crim**inate	[d'**skrɪm**'neɪt]
duplicate	[**dju:**pl'kət]	to **du**plicate	[**dju:**pl'keɪt]
e**lab**orate	[ɪ**læb**'rət]	to e**lab**orate	[ɪ**læb**'reɪt]
an **es**timate	[**est**'mət]	to **es**timate	[**est**'meɪt]
graduate	[**grædʒ**ʊət]	to **grad**uate	[**grædʒ**ueɪt]
intimate	[**int**'mət]	to **in**timate	[**int**'meɪt]
moderate	[**mɑd**əʳət]	to **mod**erate	[**mɑd**əʳeɪt]
predicate	[**pred**'kət]	to **pred**icate	[**pred**'keɪt]
separate	[**sep**'rət]	to **sep**arate	[**sep**'reɪt]

1.～14. の各文には、同じ単語が 2 度出てきます（イタリック体になっています）。文の意味を考えながら、それぞれの単語のストレスを受ける音節に（ストレス位置が同じ場合は、変化している母音部分に）下線を引いてください。音声を聞いて答えを確認した後、繰り返し発音練習をしてみましょう。

1. You need to *insert* a paragraph here on this newspaper *insert*.
2. How can you *object* to this *object*?
3. I'd like to *present* you with this *present*.
4. Would you care to *elaborate* on his *elaborate* explanation?
5. The manufacturer couldn't *recall* if there'd been a *recall*.
6. The religious *convert* wanted to *convert* the world.
7. The political *rebels* wanted to *rebel* against the world.
8. The mogul wanted to *record* a new *record* for his latest artist.
9. If you *perfect* your intonation, your accent will be *perfect*.
10. Due to the drought, the fields didn't *produce* much *produce* this year.
11. Unfortunately, City Hall wouldn't *permit* them to get a *permit*.
12. Have you heard that your *associate* is known to *associate* with gangsters?
13. How much do you *estimate* that the *estimate* will be?
14. The facilitator wanted to *separate* the general topic into *separate* categories.

3　語句のアクセント

2 語からなる語句のアクセントパターンを練習しましょう。アクセントを受ける単語は太字になっていますが、実際にアクセントを受けるのはその単語のストレス音節であることを忘れないようにしましょう。

3-1　名詞句／形容詞句

① 形容詞＋名詞
形容詞と名詞が並んだときは、原則として名詞にアクセントを置きます。

音声の後について繰り返し発音してみましょう。自分でも同じような文を作ってみましょう。

形容詞	形容詞＋名詞
1. It's **short**.	It's a short **nail**.
2. It's **chocolate**.	It's a chocolate **cake**.
3. It's **good**.	It's a good **plan**.

形容詞	形容詞＋名詞
4. It's **guarded**.	It's a guarded **gate**.
5. It's **wide**.	It's a wide **river**.
6. There're **four**.	There're four **cards**.
7. It was **small**.	It was a small **spot**.
8. It's the **best**.	It's the best **book**.
9. It's _____	It's a _____
10. It's _____	It's a _____
11. It's _____	It's a _____

② 副詞＋形容詞

副詞と形容詞が並んだときは、原則として形容詞にアクセントを置きます。

音声の後について繰り返し練習してみましょう。自分でも同じような文を作ってみましょう。

形容詞＋名詞	副詞＋形容詞
1. It's a short **nail**.	It's really **short**.
2. It's a chocolate **cake**.	It's dark **chocolate**.
3. It's a hot **bath**.	It's too **hot**.
4. It's a hard **drive**.	It's extremely **hard**.
5. It's the back **door**.	It's far **back**.
6. There are four **cards**.	There are only **four**.
7. It's a small **spot**.	It's laughably **small**.
8. It's a good **book**.	It's amazingly **good**.
9. It's a _____	It's _____
10. It's a _____	It's _____
11. It's a _____	It's _____

①と②で練習したアクセントパターンを含む文章を読んでみましょう。該当する語句はイタリック体になっていますが、2番目の単語にアクセントを置くよう注意してください。音声の後について繰り返し発音してみましょう。

There is a *mother* **duck**. She lays *three* **eggs**. Soon, there are three *baby* **birds**. Two of the birds are *very* **beautiful**. One of them is *quite* **ugly**. The *beautiful* **ducklings** make fun of their *ugly* **brother**. The *poor* **thing** is *very* **unhappy**. As the *three* **birds** grow older, the *ugly* **duckling** begins to change. His *gray* **feathers** turn *snowy* **white**. His *gangly* **neck** becomes *beautifully* **smooth**.

In *early* **spring**, the *ugly* **duckling** is swimming in a *small* **pond** in the *back* **yard** of the *old* **farm**. He sees his *shimmering* **reflection** in the *clear* **water**. What a *great* **surprise!** He is no longer an *ugly* **duckling**. He has grown into a *lovely* **swan**.

3-2 | 複合名詞

2つまたはそれ以上の単語が結びつき1単語のように使われる名詞を複合名詞と言います。〈形容詞＋名詞〉からなる普通の名詞句とは違い、複合名詞は最初の語がアクセントを受けることが多いのが特徴です。複合名詞は2語の意味を足し合わせるだけでは説明できない意味を持つ場合もあります。

greenhouse（温室）　　**high** school（高校）
darkroom（暗室）　　**eating** house（飲食店）

音声の後について繰り返し発音してみましょう。自分でも同じような文を作ってみましょう。

名詞	名詞／形容詞	複合名詞
1. It's a **finger**.	It's a **nail**.	It's a **finger**nail.
2. It's a **pan**.	It's a **cake**.	It's a **pan**cake.
3. It's a **tub**.	It's **hot**.	It's a **hot** tub.
4. It's a **drive**.	It's **hard**.	It's a **hard** drive.
5. It's a **bone**.	It's in **back**.	It's the **back**bone.
6. It's a **card**.	It's a **trick**.	It's a **card** trick.
7. It's a **spot**.	It's a **light**.	It's a **spot**light.
8. It's a **book**.	It's a **phone**.	It's a **phone** book.
9. It's a _____	It's a _____	It's a _____
10. It's a _____	It's a _____	It's a _____
11. It's a _____	It's a _____	It's a _____

絵の内容に合うよう名詞を加え、複合名詞を完成させましょう。

1. a chair   *a chairman*
2. a phone   _____
3. a house   _____
4. a base   _____
5. a door   _____
6. the White   _____
7. a movie   _____
8. the bullet   _____
9. a race   _____
10. a coffee   _____

11. a wrist   _____
12. a beer   _____
13. a high   _____
14. a hunting   _____
15. a dump   _____
16. a jelly   _____
17. a love   _____
18. a thumb   _____
19. a lightning   _____
20. a pad   _____

複合名詞を含む文章を読む練習です。最初の語にアクセントを置くよう注意してください。

The little *match* girl was out in a *snowstorm*. Her feet were like *ice cubes* and her *fingertips* had *frostbite*. She hadn't sold any matches since *daybreak*, and she had a *stomachache* from the *hunger* pangs, but her *stepmother* would beat her with a *broomstick* if she came home with an empty *coin purse*. Looking into the bright *living rooms*, she saw *Christmas* trees and warm *fireplaces*. Out on the *snowbank*, she lit match and saw the image of a grand *dinner* table of food before her. As the *matchstick* burned, the illusion slowly faded. She lit another one and saw a room full of happy *family* members. On the last match, her *grandmother* came down and carried her home. In the morning, the *passersby* saw the little *match* girl. She had frozen during the *nighttime*, but she had a smile on her face.

3-3 名詞句と複合名詞

次は名詞句と複合名詞をペアにして練習します。名詞句は2つ目の単語に、複合名詞は最初の単語にアクセントを置くのを忘れないようにしましょう。

Exercise 2-11   CD 1-23

音声の後について繰り返し発音してみましょう。

名詞句	複合名詞
1. It's a short **nail**.	It's a **finger**nail.
2. It's a chocolate **cake**.	It's a **pan**cake.
3. It's a hot **bath**.	It's a **hot** tub.
4. It's a long **drive**.	It's a **hard** drive.
5. It's the back **door**.	It's the **back**bone.
6. There are four **cards**.	It's a **card** trick.
7. It's a small **spot**.	It's a **spot**light.
8. It's a good **book**.	It's a **phone** book.

Exercise 2-12

音声の後について繰り返し発音してみましょう。

CD 1-24

名詞句	複合名詞
a light **bulb**	a **light** bulb
blue **pants**	**blue** jeans
a cold **fish**	a **gold**fish
a gray **hound**	a **grey**hound
an old **key**	an **inn** key
a white **house**	the **White** House
a nice **watch**	a **wrist**watch
a sticky **web**	a **spider** web
a clean **cup**	a **coffee** cup
a sharp **knife**	a **steak** knife
a baby **alligator**	a **baby** bottle
a shiny **tack**	**thumb**tacks
a wire **brush**	a **hair**brush
a new **ball**	a **foot**ball
a toy **gun**	a **machine** gun

名詞句	複合名詞
a silk **bow**	a **Band**-Aid
a bright **star**	a **fire** cracker

複合名詞は最初の語にアクセントを置くことが多いのですが、2番目の語に置かれる場合もあります。

CD 1-25

複合名詞
Mary **Jones**
Bob **Smith**
foreign **affairs**
down **payment**
New **York**
Social **Security**
City **Hall**

3-4 まとめ

これまでに触れなかったものも含め、2語からなる語句のアクセントパターンをまとめておきましょう。(複合語のアクセントは例外が多いので、気になるときは辞書で確認するようにしてください)。

最初の語にアクセント

■ 複合名詞	**light** bulb
■ street 名	**Main** Street
■ Co./Corp.（株式会社）	**Xerox** Corporation
■ food や people など、漠然とした意味しか持たない語が含まれるとき	**Chinese** food, **French** guy
■ 動詞＋前置詞	**look** at, **hope** for

2番目の語にアクセント

■ 名詞句	new **information**
■ avenue 名	Fifth **Avenue**
■ 副詞＋形容詞	really **big**
■ 場所の名前、公園名	New **York**, Central **Park**
■ 公共施設、Inc.（株式会社）	Oakland **Museum**, Xerox **Inc.**
■ 人名、職級	Bob **Smith**, Assistant **Manager**
■ 人称代名詞の所有格＋名詞、名詞の所有格＋名詞	his **car**, Bob's **brother**
■ 冠詞＋名詞	the **bus**, a **week**, an **hour**

2番目の語にアクセント

- 頭文字、略語   U.S., **IQ**
- 化合物   zinc **oxide**
- 色、数字   red **orange**, 26
- 動詞＋副詞   go **away**, sit **down**, fall **off**
- 割合、ドル   10 **percent**, 50 **dollars**
- ハイフンつきの国籍   African-**American**

Exercise 2-13   CD 1-26

アクセントの位置が変わると、語句の意味が変わってしまうときもあります。音声の後について繰り返し発音してみましょう。

複合名詞

An **English** teacher . . .

   . . . teaches English.

An **English** book . . .

   . . . teaches the English language.

An **English** test . . .

   . . . tests a student on the English language.

English food . . .

   . . . is kippers for breakfast.

名詞句

An English **teacher** . . .

   . . . is from England.

An English **book** . . .

   . . . is on any subject, but it came from England.

An English **test** . . .

   . . . is on any subject, but it deals with or came from England.

An English **restaurant** . . .

   . . . serves kippers for breakfast.

Exercise 2-14   CD 1-27

意味を考えながら、アクセントが置かれる単語に下線を引いてください。音声を聞いて正解を確認した後、繰り返し発音してみましょう。

1. the White House
2. a white house
3. a darkroom
4. a dark room
5. Fifth Avenue

6. Main Street
7. a main street
8. a hot dog
9. a hot dog
10. a baby blanket

11. a baby's blanket

12. a baby bird

13. a blackbird

14. a black bird

15. a greenhouse

16. a green house

17. a green thumb

18. a parking ticket

19. a one-way ticket

20. an unpaid ticket

21. convenience store

22. convenient store

23. to pick up

24. a pickup truck

25. six years old

26. a six-year-old

27. six and a half

28. a sugar bowl

29. a wooden bowl

30. a large bowl

31. a mixing bowl

32. a top hat

33. a nice hat

34. a straw hat

35. Ph.D.

36. IBM

37. MIT

38. a doorknob

39. a glass door

40. a locked door

41. the final year

42. a yearbook

43. United States

44. New York

45. Long Beach

46. Central Park

47. a raw deal

48. a deal breaker

49. the bottom line

50. a bottom feeder

太字で示された語句のうち、アクセントが置かれる単語に下線を引いてください。音声を聞いて正解を確認した後、繰り返し発音してみましょう。

1. He's a **nice guy**.

2. He's an **American guy** from **San Francisco**.

3. The **cheerleader** needs a **rubber band** to hold her **ponytail**.

4. The **executive assistant** needs a **paper clip** for the **final report**.

5. The **law student** took an **English test** in a **foreign country**.

6. The **policeman** saw a **red car** on the **freeway** in **Los Angles**.

7. My **old dog** has **long ears** and a **flea problem**.

8. The **new teacher** broke his **coffee cup** on the **first day**.

9. His **best friend** has a **broken cup** in his **other office**.

10. Let's play **football** on the **weekend** in **New York**.

11. "**Jingle Bells**" is a **nice song**.

12. Where are my **new shoes**?

13. Where are my **tennis shoes**?

14. I have a **headache** from the **heat wave** in **South Carolina**.

15. The **newlyweds** took a **long walk** in **Long Beach**.

16. The **little dog** was sitting on the **sidewalk**.

17. The **famous athlete** changed clothes in the **locker room**.

18. The **art exhibit** was held in an **empty room**.

19. There was a **class reunion** at the **high school**.

20. The **headlines** indicated a **new policy**.

21. We got **on line** and went to americanaccent **dot com**.

22. The **stock options** were listed in the **company directory**.

23. All the **second-graders** were out on the **playground**.

太字の単語にアクセントを置くことを意識して読んでみましょう。その後、音声の後について
繰り返して発音してみましょう。

There is a *little* **girl**. Her name is ***Goldilocks***. She is in a *sunny* ***forest***. She sees a *small*
house. She **knocks** on the door, but **no** *one* answers. She *goes* **inside**. In the *large* ***room***,
there are *three* **chairs**. ***Goldilocks*** sits on the **biggest** *chair*, but it is *too* **high**. She sits
on the **middle**-*sized* one, but it is *too* **low**. She sits on the **small** *chair* and it is *just* **right**.
On the table, there are *three* **bowls**. There is *hot* **porridge** in the bowls. She tries the
first *one*, but it is *too* **hot**; the **second** *one* is *too* **cold**, and the **third** *one* is *just* **right**, so
she eats it all. ***After*** *that*, she *goes* **upstairs**. She *looks* **around**. There are *three* **beds**, so
she *sits* **down**. The **biggest** *bed* is *too* **hard**. The **middle**-*sized* bed is *too* **soft**. The **little**
one is *just* **right**, so she *lies* **down**. Soon, she *falls* **asleep**. In the **meantime**, the family
of *three* **bears** comes home—the **Papa** *bear*, the **Mama** *bear*, and the **Baby** *bear*. They
look **around**. They say, "Who's been sitting in our chairs and eating our porridge?"
Then they *run* **upstairs**. They say, "Who's been sleeping in our beds?" ***Goldilocks***
wakes **up**. She is *very* **scared**. She *runs* **away**. ***Goldilocks*** never *comes* **back**.

4 文のアクセントと英語のリズム

Unit 1 で出てきた「名詞＋動詞＋名詞」の基本的なアクセントパターンをベースにし
て、英語のリズムを崩さず文を読む練習をしてみましょう。なんらかのパターンが繰
り返し起こるとき、私たちはそこにリズムを感じます。英語はストレス音節がほぼ同
じ間隔で繰り返し現れる特徴があり、これが英語独特の強弱リズムを生み出していま
す。同じリズムの文なら（＝ストレス音節の数が同じなら）、発音するのにかかる時間
はだいたい同じになります。以下の３つの文は含まれる単語の数は異なりますが、ス
トレス音節の数はどれも３つなので、発音するとだいたい同じ長さになるのです。

1)   DOGS   EAT   BONES.

2) The DOGS   will   EAT   the   BONES.

3) The DOGS will have EATen the BONES.

英語らしいリズムで話せるかどうかは、ストレスのない音節をいかに弱く、素早く発
音できるかにかかっています。ちなみに、上記の文のように名詞＋動詞＋名詞からな
る文ではアクセントは名詞に置かれ、動詞はアクセントを受けずに弱化する傾向があ
り、結果的に Unit 1 で見たような **Dogs** eat **bones**. というアクセントパターンができ
あがることになります（アクセントとリズムの関係については Unit 15 を参照）。

基本文 **Dogs** eat **bones**. のアクセントパターン ⎡‾⎤_⎡‾⎤ （強弱強）を使って練習をしてみましょう。まず、**Dogs** eat **bones**. をスムーズに言えるまで繰り返し発音してください。その後音声について 1.〜24. の各文を **Dogs** eat **bones**. と同じパターンで読めるよう何度も繰り返し練習しましょう。Dogs と bones に挟まれる単語が増えれば増えるほど発音するのが難しくなります。

＊ [t] は母音に挟まれ、2 番目の母音にストレスがない場合は [d] のような発音になります。
＊ shouldn't や couldn't の最後の [t] は、直前の [n] の影響を受けて [n] 化し、直後の母音とセットで発音されています。

eat	1. The **dogs** eat the **bones**.	[ðə **dag** zi:t ðə **boʊnz**]
ate	2. The **dogs** ate the **bones**.	[ðə **dag** zeɪt ðə **boʊnz**]
are eating	3. The **dogs**'re eating the **bones**.	[ðə **dag** zə ri:diŋ ðə **boʊnz**]
will eat	4. The **dogs**'ll eat the **bones** *(if…)*	[ðə **dag** zə li:t ðə **boʊnz**]
would eat	5. The **dogs**'d eat the **bones** *(if…)*	[ðə **dag** zə di:t ðə **boʊnz**]
would have eaten	6. The **dogs**'d've eaten the **bones** *(if…)*	[ðə **dag** zədə vi:tn ðə **boʊnz**]
that have eaten	7. The **dogs** that've eaten the **bones** *(are…)*	[ðə **dag** zədə vi:tn ðə **boʊnz**]
have eaten	8. The **dogs**'ve eaten the **bones**.	[ðə **dag** zə vi:tn ðə **boʊnz**]
had eaten	9. The **dogs**'d eaten the **bones**.	[ðə **dag** zə di:tn ðə **boʊnz**]
will have eaten	10. The **dogs**'ll've eaten the **bones**.	[ðə **dag** zələ vi:tn ðə **boʊnz**]
ought to eat	11. The **dogs** ought to eat the **bones**.	[ðə **dag** za:də i:t ðə **boʊnz**]
should eat	12. The **dogs** should eat the **bones**.	[ðə **dagz** ʃ'di:t ðə **boʊnz**]
should not eat	13. The **dogs** shouldn't eat the **bones**.	[ðə **dagz** ʃ'dn ni:t ðə **boʊnz**]
should have eaten	14. The **dogs** should've eaten the **bones**.	[ðə **dagz** ʃ'də vi:tn ðə **boʊnz**]
should not have	15. The **dogs** shouldn't have eaten the **bones**.	[ðə **dagz** ʃ'dn nə vi:tn ðə **boʊnz**]
could eat	16. The **dogs** could eat the **bones**.	[ðə **dagz** k'di:t ðə **boʊnz**]
could not eat	17. The **dogs** couldn't eat the **bones**.	[ðə **dagz** k'dn ni:t ðə **boʊnz**]
could have eaten	18. The **dogs** could've eaten the **bones**.	[ðə **dagz** k'də vi:tn ðə **boʊnz**]
could not have	19. The **dogs** couldn't've eaten the **bones**.	[ðə **dagz** k'dn nə vi:tn ðə **boʊnz**]
might eat	20. The **dogs** might eat the **bones**.	[ðə **dagz** maɪdi:t ðə **boʊnz**]
might have eaten	21. The **dogs** might've eaten the **bones**.	[ðə **dagz** maɪdəvi:tn ðə **boʊnz**]
must eat	22. The **dogs** must eat the **bones**.	[ðə **dagz** məs ti:t ðə **boʊnz**]
must have eaten	23. The **dogs** must've eaten the **bones**.	[ðə **dagz** məstəvi:tn ðə **boʊnz**]
can eat	24. The **dogs** can eat the **bones**.	[ðə **dagz** k'ni:t ðə **boʊnz**]

今度は「代名詞＋動詞＋代名詞」のアクセントパターン ＿⌐¬＿ （弱強弱）を使って同じような練習をしてみましょう。まず、基本文 They **eat** them. をスムーズに言えるまで繰り返し発音してください。アクセントを置くのは eat だけです。その後、音声の後について 1. 〜 24. の各文を They **eat** them. と同じパターンで発音できるよう何度も繰り返し練習してください。

＊ them の最初の音 [ð]，および him や her の最初の音 [h] はストレスがないと消えてしまうことがあります。

present	1. They **eat** them.	[ðeɪ **i:**d'm]
past	2. They **ate** them.	[ðeɪ **eɪ**d'm]
countinuous	3. They're **eating** them.	[ðə **ri:**diŋ'm]
future	4. They'll **eat** them (if...)	[ðə **li:**d'm]
present conditional	5. They'd **eat** them (if...)	[ðeɪ **di:**d'm]
past conditional	6. They'd've **eaten** them (if...)	[ðeɪ də**vi:**tn'm]
relative pronoun	7. The ones that've **eaten** them (are...)	[ðə wən zədə**vi:**tn'm]
present perfect	8. They've **eaten** them (many times).	[ðeɪ **vi:**tn'm]
past perfect	9. They'd **eaten** them (before...)	[ðeɪ **di:**tn'm]
future perfect	10. They'll have **eaten** them (by...)	[ðeɪ lə**vi:**tn'm]
obligation	11. They ought to **eat** them.	[ðeɪ ɑ:də **i:**d'm]
obligation	12. They should **eat** them.	[ðeɪ ʃ**di:**d'm]
obligation	13. They shouldn't **eat** them.	[ðeɪ ʃdn **ni:**d'm]
obligation	14. They should have **eaten** them.	[ðeɪ ʃdə**vi:**tn'm]
obligation	15. They shouldn't've **eaten** them.	[ðeɪ ʃdn nə**vi:**tn'm]
possibility/ability	16. They could **eat** them.	[ðeɪ k'**di:**d'm]
possibility/ability	17. They couldn't **eat** them.	[ðeɪ k'dn **ni:**d'm]
possibility/ability	18. They could have **eaten** them.	[ðeɪ k'də **vi:**tn'm]
possibility/ability	19. They couldn't have **eaten** them.	[ðeɪ k'dn nə **vi:**tn'm]
possibility	20. They might **eat** them.	[ðeɪ maɪ**di:**d'm]
possibility	21. They might have **eaten** them.	[ðeɪ maɪdə**vi:**tn'm]
probability	22. They must **eat** them.	[ðeɪ məs **ti:**d'm]
probability	23. They must have **eaten** them.	[ðeɪ məstə**vi:**tn'm]
ability	24. They can **eat** them.	[ðeɪ k'**ni:**d'm]

今度は３つの単語にアクセントが置かれた文を使って同じような練習をしてみます。音声の後
について繰り返し発音してみましょう。強い音節がほぼ等間隔になるよう弱い部分を素早く発
音するよう心がけてください。

1. The **dogs** eat the **bones** every **day**.   [ð' **dag** ziːt ð' **boʊnz**evri **deɪ**]

2. The **dogs** ate the **bones** last **week**.   [ð' **dag** zeɪt ð' **boʊnz**læs **twiːk**]

3. The **dogs**'re eating the **bones** right **now**. [ð' **dag** zə riːdiŋ ð' **boʊnz** raɪt **naʊ**]

4. The **dogs**'ll eat the **bones** if they're **here**. [ð' **dag** zə liːt ð' **boʊnz**if ðeəʳ **hɪəʳ**]

5. The **dogs**'d eat the **bones** if they were **here**. [ð' **dag** zə diːt ð' **boʊnz**if ðeɪ wəʳ **hɪəʳ**]

6. The **dogs**'d've eaten the **bones** if they'd **been** here. [ð' **dag** zədə viːtn ð' **boʊnz**if ðeɪd **bin** hɪəʳ]

7. The **dogs** that've eaten the **bones** are **sick**. [ð' **dag** zədə viːtn ð' **boʊnz**əʳ **sɪk**]

8. The **dogs**'ve eaten the **bones** every **day**.   [ð' **dag** zə viːtn ð' **boʊnz**evri **deɪ**]

9. The **dogs**'d eaten the **bones** by the time we **got** there. [ð' **dag** zə diːtn ð' **boʊnz** baɪ ð' taɪm wi **gat** ðeəʳ]

10. The **dogs**'ll have eaten the **bones** by the time we **get** there. [ð' **dag** zələ viːtn ð' **boʊnz** baɪ ð' taɪm wi **get** ðeəʳ]

以下のペアは Exercise 2-17 で練習した文です。各ペアは音声的にはとても似ていますが、意
味は全く違うので、リスニングのときは特に注意が必要です。音声をよく聞き、その後、繰り
返し発音してみましょう。

would eat	5. The **dogs**'d eat the **bones**.	その犬ならあの骨を食べるだろう。
had eaten	9. The **dogs**'d eaten the **bones**.	（飼い主が帰宅する前に）その犬はあの骨を食べてしまっていた。
would have eaten	6. The **dogs**'d've eaten the **bones**.	その犬ならあの骨を食べていただろう。
that have eaten	7. The **dogs** that've eaten the **bones**.	その骨を食べたばかりの犬
will eat	4. The **dogs**'ll eat the **bones**.	その犬はあの骨を食べるだろう。
would eat	5. The **dogs**'d eat the **bones**.	その犬ならあの骨を食べるだろう。
would have eaten	6. The **dogs**'d've eaten the **bones**.	その犬ならあの骨を食べていただろう。
have eaten	8. The **dogs**'ve eaten the **bones**.	その犬はあの骨を食べてしまった。
had eaten	9. The **dogs**'d eaten the **bones**.	その犬はあの骨を食べてしまっていた。
will have eaten	10. The **dogs**'ll've eaten the **bones**.	その犬はあの骨を食べてしまっているだろう。

would eat	5.	The **dogs**'d eat the **bones**.	その犬ならあの骨を食べるだろう。
ought to eat	11.	The **dogs** ought to eat the **bones**.	その犬はあの骨を食べるべきだ。

Exercise 2-21 CD 1-34

次は can と can't の区別をする練習をしてみましょう。肯定文では can は [k'n] と弱く発音され、動詞がアクセントを受けます。否定文では、can't を [kæn⁽ᵗ⁾] とかなり短く発音し、can't と動詞両方にアクセントを置きます。can を強調する場合は [kæn] の母音部分を 2 倍に伸ばすつもりでアクセントを置いて発音し、動詞にはアクセントを置きません。can't を強調する場合は、その後の動詞にはアクセントを置きません。繰り返し発音してみましょう。

I can **do** it.	[aɪ k'n **du:** ɪt]	（肯定文）
I **can't** do it.	[aɪ **kæn⁽ᵗ⁾du:** ɪt]	（否定文）
I **can** do it.	[aɪ **kææn** du: ɪt]	（強調）
I **can't** do it.	[aɪ **kæn⁽ᵗ⁾du:** ɪt]	（否定の強調）

Exercise 2-22

再び基本文をベースに文をどんどん長くしていきましょう。リズムを崩さないよう何度も練習してみましょう。

CD 1-35

1. I bought a **sand**wich.
2. I **said** I bought a **sand**wich.
3. I **said** I think I bought a **sand**wich.
4. I said I **really** think I bought a **sand**wich.
5. I said I **really** think I bought a chicken **sand**wich.
6. I said I **really** think I bought a **chicken** salad **sand**wich.
7. I said I **really** think I bought a **half** a chicken salad **sand**wich.
8. I said I **really** think I bought a **half** a chicken salad **sand**wich this after**noon**.
9. I **actually** said I **really** think I bought a **half** a chicken salad **sand**wich this after**noon**.
10. I **actually** said I **really** think I bought another **half** a chicken salad **sand**wich this after**noon**.
11. Can you **believe** I **actually** said I **really** think I bought another **half** a chicken salad **sand**wich this after**noon**?

1. I **did** it.

2. I did it **again**.

3. I already **did** it again.

4. I think I already **did** it again.

5. I **said** I think I already **did** it again.

6. I **said** I think I already **did** it again **yesterday**.

7. I **said** I think I already **did** it again the day before **yesterday**.

1. I want a **ball**.

2. I want a large **ball**.

3. I want a **large**, red **ball**.

4. I want a **large**, red, bouncy **ball**.

5. I want a **large**, red, bouncy rubber **ball**.

6. I want a **large**, red, bouncy rubber **basket**ball.

1. I want a **raise**.

2. I want a big **raise**.

3. I want a **big**, impressive **raise**.

4. I want a **big**, impressive, annual **raise**.

5. I want a **big**, impressive, annual cost of **living** raise.

5 弱く発音される単語

文の中では特に理由がない限り、弱く発音される単語をまとめて取り上げます。このような単語は、単独で発音されるとき（強形）と文中に出てきたとき（弱形）とでは母音（や子音）の発音が変わるときがあります。まずは冠詞から見てみましょう。

Exercise 2-23 CD 1-39

冠詞の the は次に続く単語が子音で始まるときは [ðə] となり、母音で始まるときは [ði(ː)] になります。音声の後について発音してみましょう。

子音	母音
the man	the apple
the best	the egg
the last one	the easy way

冠詞の a は、次に続く単語が子音で始まるときは [ə]、母音で始まるときは an [ən] になります。このときの発音に注意してください。an の [n] の音は次の単語の最初の音であるかのように発音します。an ugly hat は [ən ʌgli hæt]（アン・アグリー・ハット）ではなく [ə nʌgli hæt]（ア・ナグリー・ハット）のように発音するのです（詳しくは Unit 3 を参照）。音声の後について発音してみましょう。

＊ interview の [t] は発音するときの発音位置（舌の位置）がその前の [n] と似ているため消えたように聞こえます（Unit 3、Unit 5 を参照）。

子音	母音
a girl	an orange [ə nɑrındʒ]
a banana	an opening [ə noʊpnıŋ]
a computer	an interview [ə nınəʳvju:]

他にも代名詞、前置詞、接続詞、助動詞などは通常弱く発音され、ストレスを受けません。

Exercise 2-24

音声の後について自然に発音できるようになるまで繰り返し練習してみましょう。

＊ (t)/(d) は [t]/[d] を発音する口の構えだけ作って息は吐き出さず、そのまま次の音に移行することを表しています（詳しくは Unit 5 を参照）。文末に来る [t]/[d] も通常この発音ですが、以下の練習問題では煩雑さを避けるために普通の表記にしてあります。
＊ 発音記号も書いてありますが、大切なのは音声の後について正確に繰り返すことです。

CD 1-40	文字では…	発音は…
To [tu:] → [t' / tə]	to work	[t'**wəʳ:k**]
	to school	[t'**sku:l**]
	to the store	[t' ð' **stɔəʳ**]
	We have to go now.	[wi hæftə **goʊ** naʊ]
	He went to work.	[hi wentə **wəʳ:k**]
	They hope to find it.	[ðeɪ hoʊptə **faɪn** dɪt]
	I can't wait to find out.	[aɪ **kæn**(t)weɪ(t)tə faɪn **daʊt**]
	We don't know what to do.	[wi doʊn(t)noʊ w'(t)t' **du:**]
	Don't jump to conclusions.	[doʊn(t)dʒ'm t' k'n**klu:**ʒ'nz]
	To be or not to be . . .	[t' **bi:**əʳ **nɑ**(t)t' bi:]
	He didn't get to go.	[hi dɪn(t)ge(t)tə **goʊ**]

文字では…	発音は…

前に母音などの有声音
があるときは
[d' / də]

He told me to help.	[hi toʊld miːdə **help**]
She told you to get it.	[ʃi toʊl dʒuːdə **ge**dɪt]
I go to work.	[aɪ goʊdə **wəᵣːk**]
The only way to get it is . . .	[ðiːoʊnli weɪdə **ge**dɪdɪz]
You've got to pay to get it.	[juːv gadə peɪdə **ge**dɪt]
We plan to do it.	[wi plæn də **duː** ɪt]
Let's go to lunch.	[lets goʊdə **lʌntʃ**]
The score was 4-6.	[ð' skɔəᵣ w'z fɔəᵣ də **sɪks**]
It's the only way to do it.	[ɪts ðiːoʊnli weɪdə **duː**'t]
So to speak . . .	[soʊdə **spiːk**]
I don't know how to say it.	[aɪ doʊn⁽ᵗ⁾noʊ haʊdə **seɪ**ɪt]
Go to page 8.	[goʊdə peɪ **dʒeɪt**]
Show me how to get it.	[ʃoʊ mi haʊdə **ge**dɪt]
You need to know when to do it.	[ju niː⁽ᵈ⁾də noʊ wendə **duː**ɪt]
Who's to blame?	[huːz də **bleɪm**]

CD 1-41

At
[æt] → [ət / 't]

We're at home.	[wiəᵣət **hoʊm**]
I'll see you at lunch.	[aɪl siː juət **lʌntʃ**]
Dinner's at five.	[dɪnəᵣzət **faɪv**]
Leave them at the door.	[liːv'm'⁽ᵗ⁾ð' **dɔəᵣ**]
The meeting's at one.	[ð' miːdɪŋ z't **wʌn**]
He's at the post office.	[hiːz'⁽ᵗ⁾ðə **poʊs**taːfəs]
They're at the bank.	[ðeəᵣ'⁽ᵗ⁾ð' **bæŋk**]
I'm at school.	[aɪmə⁽ᵗ⁾**skuːl**]

後に母音があるときは
['d / əd]

I'll see you at eleven.	[aɪl siː juədə **lev**'n]
He's at a meeting.	[hiːz'də **miː**dɪŋ]
She laughed at his idea.	[ʃi læf dədɪ zaɪ **diːə**]
one at a time	[wənədə **taɪm**]
We got it at an auction.	[wi gadɪdədə **naːk**ʃ'n]
The show started at eight.	[ð' ʃoʊ staəᵣtədə **deɪt**]
The dog jumped out at us.	[ð' dag dʒʌmp **taʊ** dədəs]

CD 1-42	文字では…	発音は…
It	Can you do it?	[k'nju du:'t]
[ɪt] → ['t]	Give it to me.	[g'v'⁽ᵗ⁾t' mi]
	Buy it tomorrow,	[baɪ'⁽ᵗ⁾t' mɑroʊ]
	It can wait.	['t k'n weɪt]
	Read it twice.	[ri: d'⁽ᵗ⁾twaɪs]
	Forget about it!	[fəʳged' baʊdɪt]
後に母音があるときは	Give it a try.	[gɪvɪdə traɪ]
['d / ɪd]	Let it alone.	[ledɪdə loʊn]
	Take it away.	[teɪ kɪdə weɪ]
	I got it in London.	[aɪ gɑdɪdɪn lʌnd'n]
	What is it about?	[w'd'z'd'baʊt]
CD 1-43		
For	This is for you.	[ð's'z fəʳ ju:]
	It's for my friend.	['ts fəʳ maɪ frend]
	A table for four, please.	[ə teɪbl fəʳ fɔəʳ pli:z]
	We planned it for later.	[wi plæn dɪt fəʳ leɪdəʳ]
	for example, for instance	[fəʳɪg zæmpl] [fəʳɪn st'ns]
	What is this for?	[w'd'z ðɪs fɔəʳ]
	What did you do it for?	[w'dʒ' du:ɪt fɔəʳ]
	Who did you get it for?	[hu:dʒə gedɪt fɔəʳ]
CD 1-44		
From	It's from the IRS.	['ts fr'm ði aɪɑəʳ res]
	I'm from Arkansas.	[aɪm fr'm ɑəʳk'nsɑ:]
	There's a letter from Bob.	[ðeəʳzə ledəʳ fr'm bɑb]
	This letter's from Alaska!	[ðɪs ledəʳz frəmə læskə]
	Who's it from?	[hu:zɪt frəm]
	Where are you from?	[weəʳəʳ ju frəm]
CD 1-45		
In	It's in the bag.	['tsɪn ðə bæg]
	What's in it?	[w'ts'n't]
	I'll be back in a minute.	[aɪl bi bæk'nə m'n't]
	This movie? Who's in it?	[ðɪs mu:vi hu:z'n't]
	Come in.	[k'mɪn]
	He's in America.	[hi:z'nə merəkə]

CD 1-46	文字では…	発音は…

An

He's an American.	[hi:z'nə **mer**əkən]
I got an A in English.	[aɪ gɑdə **neɪ** ɪnɪŋglɪʃ]
He got an F in Algebra.	[hi: gɑdə **nef** ɪnældʒəbrə]
He had an accident.	[hi hædə **næk**səd'nt]
We want an orange.	[wi want'n **nɑr**ɪndʒ]
He didn't have an excuse.	[hi dɪdn⁽ᵗ⁾hævə neks **kju:s**]
I'll be there in an instant.	[aɪl bi ðeəʳ ɪnə **nɪn**st'nt]
It's an easy mistake to make.	['tsə **ni:**zi m'steɪk t' **meɪk**]

CD 1-47		

And

ham and eggs	[hæmə **negz**]
bread and butter	[bredn **bʌd**əʳ]
Coffee? With cream and sugar?	[**kɑfi** wɪð kri:m'n **ʃʊg**əʳ]
No, lemon and sugar.	[**noʊ** lem'n'n **ʃʊg**əʳ]
. . . And some more cookies?	['n smɔəʳ **kʊkiz**]
They kept going back and forth.	[ðeɪ **kep**⁽ᵗ⁾goʊɪŋ bæk'n **fɔəʳθ**]
We watched it again and again.	[wi **watʃ** tɪt' **gen**'n' **gen**]
He did it over and over.	[hi dɪ dɪ **doʊv**əʳə **noʊv**əʳ]
We learned by trial and error.	[wi ləʳ:nd baɪ traɪəl **əner**əʳ]

CD 1-48		

Or

Soup or salad?	[su:pəʳ **sæl**əd]
now or later	[naʊəʳ **leɪd**əʳ]
more or less	[**mɔ**ʳəʳ les]
left or right	[**left**əʳ **raɪt**]
For here or to go?	[fəʳ **hɪə**ʳəʳ d'**goʊ**]
Are you going up or down?	[əʳ ju goʊɪŋ **ʌp**əʳ **daʊn**]

CD 1-49		

Are

What are you doing?	[w'dəʳ ju **du:**ɪŋ]
Where are you going?	[weəʳəʳ ju **goʊ**ɪŋ]
What're you planning on doing?	[w'dəʳ ju plænɪŋ an **du:**ɪŋ]
How are you?	[haʊəʳ **ju:**]
Those are no good.	[ðoʊzəʳ noʊ **gʊd**]
How are you doing?	[haʊəʳ ju **du:**ɪŋ]
The kids are still asleep.	[ðə **kɪd**zəʳ stɪlə **sli:p**]

CD 1-50	文字では…	発音は…
Your	How's your family?	[haʊʒəʳ **fæm**li]
	Where are your keys?	[weəʳəʳ jəʳ **ki:z**]
	You're American, aren't you?	[jəʳə **mer**'k'n ɑəʳn tʃu:]
	Tell me when you're ready.	[tel mi wen jəʳ **red**i]
	Is this your car?	[ɪzɪs jəʳ **kɑəʳ**]
	You're late again, Bob.	[jəʳ leɪ də **gen** bɑb]
	Which one is yours?	[wɪtʃ wʌn'z **j'əʳz**]

CD 1-51		
One	Which one is better?	[wɪtʃ wʌn'z **bedəʳ**]
	One of them is broken.	[wʌn'v'm'z **broʊkn̩**]
	I'll use the other one.	[aɪl ju:z ðiʌðəʳ wən]
	I like the red one, Edwin.	[aɪ laɪk ðə **red**wən edwən]
	That's the last one.	[ðæts ð' læs **twʌn**]
	The next one'll be better.	[ðə **neks** tw'n'l bi **bedəʳ**]
	Here's one for you.	[**hɪəʳ** zwʌn fəʳ **ju:**]
	Let them go one by one.	[led'm goʊ **wʌn** baɪ **wʌn**]

CD 1-52		
The	It's the best.	['ts ð' **best**]
	What's the matter?	[w'ts ð' **mætəʳ**]
	What's the problem?	[w'ts ð' **prɑ**bl'm]
	I have to go to the bathroom.	[aɪ hæf t' goʊ d' ð' **bæθ**ru:m]
	Who's the boss around here?	[hu:zə **bɑ** səraʊnd hɪəʳ]
	Give it to the dog.	[g'v'ᵗtu ð' **dɑg**]
	Put it in the drawer.	[pʊdɪdɪn ð' **drɔəʳ**]

CD 1-53		
A	It's a present.	['tsə **prez**'nt]
	You need a break.	[ju ni:də **breɪk**]
	Give him a chance.	[g'v'mə **tʃæns**]
	Let's get a new pair of shoes.	[lets getə nju: peəʳə **ʃu:z**]
	Can I have a Coke, please?	[k'naɪ hævə **kouk** pli:z]
	Is that a computer?	[ɪzædə k'm**pju:**dəʳ]
	Where's a public telephone?	[weəʳzə pʌblɪk **tel**əfoʊn]

Of

文字では…	発音は…
It's the top of the line.	['ts ð' tɑp'v ð' **laɪn**]
It's a state-of-the-art printer.	['tsə **steɪtə**ðiɑə**ᵣ⁽ᵗ⁾prɪn**tə**ᵣ**]
As a matter of fact, . . .	['z'**mæd**ə**ᵣə fækt**]
Get out of here.	[ge**dɑʊ** də hɪə**ᵣ**]
Practice all of the time.	[**præk**t's ɑ:l'v ð' taɪm]
Today's the first of May.	[t'**deɪz** ð' fə**ᵣ**:s t'v **meɪ**]
What's the name of that movie?	[w'ts ð' **neɪ** m'v ðæt **mu:vi**]
That's the best of all!	[**ðæts** ð' bes t'**vɑ:l**]
some of them	[**sʌm**əvəm]
all of them	[**ɑ:l**əvəm]
most of them	[**moʊst**əvəm]
none of them	[**nʌn**əvəm]
any of them	[**eni**əvəm]
the rest of them	[ð' **rest**əvəm]

Can

Can you speak English?	[k'nju: spi: **kɪŋ**glɪʃ]
I can only do it on Wednesday.	[aɪ k'**noʊn**li du:ɪdan **wenz**deɪ]
A can opener can open cans.	[ə **kæn**oʊpnə**ᵣ** k'**noʊ**pn **kænz**]
Can I help you?	[k'naɪ **hel** pju]
Can you do it?	[k'nju **du:**'t]
We can try it later.	[wi k'n **traɪ** ɪt **leɪ**də**ᵣ**]
I hope you can sell it.	[aɪ **hoʊ** pju k'n **sel**'t]
No one can fix it.	[noʊ w'n k'n **fɪk** sɪt]
Let me know if you can find it.	[lemi noʊ'fju k'n **faɪn** dɪt]

Had

Jack had had enough.	[dʒæk'd hæd '**nʌf**]
Bill had forgotten again.	[bɪl'd fə**ᵣ**gɑ⁽ᵗ⁾nə **gen**]
What had he done to deserve it?	[w'd'di: d'nd' d'**zə**ᵣ: vɪt]
We'd already seen it.	[wi:dɑl redi **si:** nɪt]
He'd never been there.	[hi:d nevə**ᵣ bin** ðeə**ᵣ**]
Had you ever had one?	[h'dʒu evə**ᵣ hæd**wʌn]
Where had he hidden it?	[weə**ᵣ** di: **hɪd**n nɪt]
Bob said he'd looked into it.	[bɑb sedi:d **lʊk**tɪn tʊɪt]

CD 1-57

Would

文字では…	発音は…
He would have helped, if . . .	[hi wʊdə **help** tɪf]
Would he like one?	[wʊdi **laɪ** kwʌn]
Do you think he'd do it?	[dju θɪŋ ki:d **du:'**t]
Why would I tell her?	[hwaɪ wʊdaɪ **telə**ʳ]
We'd see it again, if . . .	[wi:d si:ɪtə**gen** ɪf]
He'd never be there on time.	[hi:d nevə**ʳ bi:** ðeəʳan taɪm]
Would you ever have one?	[w'dʒu evə**ʳ hæv**wʌn]

CD 1-58

Was

He was only trying to help.	[hi w'zoʊnli traɪɪŋ də **help**]
Mark was American.	[**mɑə**ʳ kw'z'**mer**'k'n]
Where was it?	[weə**ʳ w'z'**t]
How was it?	[haʊ**w'z'**t]
That was great!	[ðæt w'z **greɪt**]
Who was with you?	[hu:**w'z wɪð** ju]
She was very clear.	[ʃi: w'z veri **klɪə**ʳ]
When was the war of 1812?	[wen w'z ð' **wɔə**ʳ**'**v eɪti:n **twelv**]

CD 1-59

What

What time is it?	[w'⁽ᵗ⁾**taɪ** m'z't]
What's up?	[w'**ts'p**]
What's on your agenda?	[w'tsɑnjəʳə **dʒen**də]
What do you mean?	[w'd'j' **mi:n**]
What did you mean?	[w'dʒ' **mi:n**]
What did you do about it?	[w'dʒ' **du:** əbaʊdɪt]
What took so long?	[w'⁽ᵗ⁾**tʊk** soʊ lɑŋ]
What do you think of this?	[w'djə θɪŋ k'v **ðɪs**]
What did you do then?	[w'dʒu du: **ðen**]
I don't know what he wants.	[aɪ doʊnt noʊ wədi: **wants**]

CD 1-60

Some

Some are better than others.	[sʌmə**ʳ** bedə**ʳ** ðə **nʌðə**ʳz]
There are some leftovers.	[ðeəʳə**ʳ** s'm **lef** toʊvə**ʳ**z]
Let's buy some ice cream.	[let spaɪ s'**maɪs** kri:m]
Could we get some other ones?	[k'dwi: get s'**mʌðə**ʳ wʌnz]
Take some of mine.	[**teɪk** səməv **maɪn**]
Would you like some more?	[w'dʒu: laɪk s'**mɔə**ʳ]
(or very casually)	[dʒlaɪk **smɔə**ʳ]
Do you have some ice?	[dju hæv sə**maɪs**]
Do you have some mice?	[dju hæv sə**maɪs**]

that は関係代名詞、接続詞として使われるときは弱く [ðə] と発音されますが、指示代名詞・形容詞のときは [ðæ] と発音されます。スピードが早いときは [ðə] が脱落することもあります。音声の後について繰り返してみましょう。

① 関係代名詞   The **car** that she ordered is **red**.

                         [ðə **kɑɚ** ð't ʃi ɔɚˈdɚ dɪz **red**]

② 接続詞   He said that he **liked** it.

                         [hi sed ðə di: **laɪk** dɪt]

③ 指示代名詞   Why did you **do** that?

                         [hwaɪ dɪdʒu: **du:** ðæt]

④ ①、②、③の組み合わせ   I **know** that he'll read that **book** that I **told** you about.

                         [aɪ **noʊ** ðə dil ri:d ðæt **bʊk** ðə daɪ **toʊld**ʒu: 'baʊt]

例にならって、弱く発音される母音に斜線を入れてください。to, for, and, that, than, the, a, 母音の [ɪ]、ストレスのない音節の母音は弱く発音されます。

Hello, **my** name is Ann. I'm taking American **Acc**ent Training. There's a **lot** to learn, but I **hope** to make it as en**joy**able as possible. I should pick **up** on the American into**na**tion pattern pretty **ea**sily, although the **on**ly way to **get** it is to **prac**tice all of the time. I use the **up** and down, or **peaks** and valleys, into**na**tion more than I **used** to. I've been paying attention to **pitch**, **too**. It's like **walk**ing down a **stair**case. I've been **talk**ing to a lot of A**mer**icans lately, and they tell me that I'm **ea**sier to under**stand**. **Any**way, I could go **on** and on, but the im**por**tant thing is to **lis**ten well and sound **good**. **Well**, what do you **think**? **Do** I?

アポストロフィーは弱い母音が省略されたことを示しています。音声の後について何度も繰り返し発音してみましょう。

  H'llo, **my** name's Ann. I'm tak'ng 'mer'c'n **Acc**'nt Train'ng. There's' **lott'** learn, b't I **hope** t' make 't's 'n**joy**'bl's poss'ble. I sh'd p'ck **'p** on the 'mer'k'n 'nt'**nati**'n pattern pretty **ea**s'ly, although the **on**ly way t' **get** 't 's t' **prac**t'ce all 'f th' time. I use the **'p**'n down, or **peaks** 'n valleys, 'nt'**nati**'n more th'n I **used** to. I've b'n pay'ng 'ttenti'n t' **p'ch**, **too**. 'Ts like **walk**'ng down' **stair**case. I've b'n **talk**'ng to' lot 'f**mer**'c'ns lately, 'n they tell me th't I'm **ea**sier to 'nder**stand**. **Any**way, I k'd go **on** 'n on, b't the 'm**por**t'nt th'ng 's t' **l's**'n wel'n sound **g'd**. **W'll**, wh'd'y' **th'nk**? **Do** I?

6 | アイデアグループ

  いくら英語らしいリズムで話せるようになっても、一本調子でただ話し続けるだけでは聞き手は話についていけません。メッセージをうまく伝えるには、コンマやピリオド以外にも適当な意味単位でポーズを置き、聞き手の理解を促す必要があります。この単位をアイデアグループ（idea group）と言います。アイデアグループはなんらかの意味を持った単語の集まり（word group）で、決まった長さはありませんが、およそ一息で発音できる単位（breath group）と一致します。語句、節、文など文法的単位ともよく重なります。具体的に見てみましょう。

音声の後について発音してみましょう。

発言	**Dogs** eat **bones**.
節	**Dogs** eat **bones**, / but **cats** eat **fish**. *or* As we all **know**, / **dogs** eat **bones**.
リスト	**Dogs** eat **bones**, / **kibbles**, / and **meat**.
質問	Do **dogs** eat **bones**?
質問の繰り返し	Do **dogs** eat **bones**?!!
付加疑問	**Dogs** eat **bones**, / **don't** they?（最後に声を上げる） **Dogs** eat **bones**, / **don't** they!（最後に声を下げる）
間接発話	He asked / if **dogs** ate **bones**.
直接発話	"Do **dogs** eat **bones**?"/ he **asked**.

以下の文章をアイデアグループに区切ってみましょう。ポーズを入れた方がよいと思うところに斜線を入れてみてください。

Hello, **my** name is Ann. I'm taking American **Accent** Training. There's a **lot** to learn, but I **hope** to make it as **enjoyable** as possible. I should pick **up** on the American **intonation** pattern pretty **easily**, although the **only** way to **get** it is to **practice** all of the time. I use the **up** and down, or **peaks** and valleys, **intonation** more than I **used** to. I've been paying attention to **pitch**, **too**. It's like **walking** down a **stair**case. I've been **talking** to a lot of **Americans** lately, and they tell me that I'm **easier** to under**stand**. **Any**way, I could go **on** and on, but the **important** thing is to **listen** well and sound **good**. **Well**, what do you **think**? **Do** I?

音声には各アイデアグループを強調するため、やや大げさなポーズが入れてあります。各ポーズの後に音声を止め、繰り返してみましょう。最後は、ポーズを自然な長さにして、アイデアグループを意識しながら何度も文章を読んでみましょう。

Hello, / **my** name is Ann. / I'm taking American **Accent** Training. / There's a **lot** to learn, / but I **hope** to make it / as **enjoyable** as possible. / I should pick **up** on / the American **intonation** pattern / pretty **easily**, / although / the **only** way to **get** it is / to **practice** all of the time. / I use the **up** and down, / or **peaks** and valleys, **intonation** / more than I **used** to. / I've been paying attention to **pitch**, / **too**. / It's like **walking** down a **stair**case. / I've been **talking** / to a lot of **Americans** / lately, / and they tell me / that I'm **easier** / to under**stand**. / **Any**way, / I could go **on** and on, / but the **important** thing is / to **listen** well / and sound **good**. / **Well**, / what do you **think**? / **Do** I?

UNIT 3

ナチュラルな発音をめざして

ネイティブスピーカーは英語を話すとき、単語単位で発音しているわけではありません。たとえば、

> They tell me that I'm easier to understand.

と書くと、まるで単語ごとにポーズを置いて発音しているように見えますが、実際は

> TheytellmethatI'measiertounderstand.

のように、They から understand までを、まるで1つの単語のように発音します。このユニットでは単語より大きい語句や文単位で英語をスムーズに発音する練習をします。

1 つながる音（音の連結）

英語では、子音で終わる単語の後に母音で始まる単語が続くとき、その子音と母音をくっつけて発音するのが普通です。たとえば、Take it easy. であれば、[teɪk ɪt iːzi]（テイク・イット・イーズィー）ではなく、[teɪ kɪ tiːzi]（テイ・キ・ティーズィー）のような発音になります。このような現象を「音の連結」と言います。

Exercise 3-1   CD 1-65

音声をよく聞いて、その後について繰り返し練習してみましょう。

My na**me i**s . . .	[maɪneɪ mɪz]	(×) [maɪ neɪm ɪz]
becau**se I**'ve	[b'k' zaɪv]	(×) [b'k'z aɪv]
pi**ck up o**n the America**n i**ntonation	[pɪkʌ pɑn ði əmer'k nɪntəneɪʃən]	
	(×) [pɪk ʌp ɑn ði əmer'kn ɪntəneɪʃən]	
LA (= Los Angles)	[e leɪ]	(×) [el eɪ]
902-5050（電話番号）	[naɪ noʊ tuː faɪ voʊ faɪ voʊ]	
	(×) [naɪn oʊ tuː faɪv oʊ faɪv oʊ]	

例を参考に、1.〜10.の語句の発音を、発音記号またはカタカナで書いてみましょう。him と her の [h] はナチュラルスピードの英語では普通発音されません。最後に音声の後について繰り返し発音してみましょう。

例

hold on	→	[hoʊl dɑn]	（ホウル・ドン）
turn over	→	[təˀː noʊvəˀ]	（ター・ノウヴァー）
tell her I miss her	→	[telə̲ˀ aɪ mɪsə̲ˀ]	（テラー・アイ・ミサー）

---

1. read only → [　　　　] （　　　　　　　）
2. fall off → [　　　　] （　　　　　　　）
3. follow up on → [　　　　] （　　　　　　　）
4. come in → [　　　　] （　　　　　　　）
5. call him → [　　　　] （　　　　　　　）
6. sell it → [　　　　] （　　　　　　　）
7. take out → [　　　　] （　　　　　　　）
8. fade away → [　　　　] （　　　　　　　）
9. 6-0 → [　　　　] （　　　　　　　）
10. MA → [　　　　] （　　　　　　　）

2 消える音・歩み寄る音（音の脱落）

英語では同じような子音が連続すると、最初の子音が消えてしまうことがよくあります。ここで言う「同じ」というのは、主に発音するときの舌の位置や口の構え（＝発音位置）、そして、息の出し方のことです。似ていれば似ているほど消えてしまう可能性は高くなります。子音の中には、[p] と [b] や [t] と [d] のように、発音位置、息の出し方が全く同じで、発音するときに声帯が振動しないか（＝無声音）、振動するか（＝有声音）だけで区別されるものもあります。(無声音と有声音についてはUnit 4を参照)。

音声の後について各子音を発音してみましょう。左から右に向かって発音されています。

発音位置／声帯の振動	無声音	有声音
唇	p	b
	f	v
	—	m
	—	w

歯茎部・硬口蓋 （上の歯の後ろとその奥）	t	d
	tʃ	dʒ
	—	l
	—	n
	s	z
	ʃ	ʒ
	—	j
のどの奥 （口の天井の後方と声帯）	k	g
	h	—
	—	ŋ
	—	r

下線部で音の脱落が起こっています。音声の後について発音してみましょう。（発音記号内の斜線は単語の切れ目を示していますが、読むときは最後まで一息に発音してください）。

I just **d**idn't get the chance.   [aɪ/dʒʌs/dɪdnt/ge⁽ᵗ⁾/ðə/tʃæns]

I've been la**te t**wice.   [aɪv/bin/leɪ/twaɪs]

TH の音 [θ]/[ð] は舌先を上下の歯の間から少し突き出して発音しますが（詳しくは、Unit 10 を参照）、その前後に歯茎（＝上の歯の後ろ）音があるときは、お互いにその影響を受けて、[θ]/[ð] は舌先が少し後ろに下がり、隣接する音は [θ]/[ð] の舌の位置に近づきます。音声をよく聞き、繰り返してみましょう。

th + l	with lemon
th + n	with nachos
th + t	both times
th + d	with delivery
th + s	both sizes
th + z	with zeal
th + ch	both charges
th + j	with juice
n + th	in the
z + th	was that
d + th	hid those

Exercise 3-6　　　　　　　　　　　　　　　　　　　　　　CD 1-70

1.～10. までの各語句は、単語の切れ目で子音が並んでいます。それぞれの子音の発音位置を確認してください。同じような子音が続くときは、最初の音が脱落することがあります。その後、音声をよく聞いて繰り返し発音してみましょう。

1. business deal
2. credit check
3. the top file
4. sell nine new cars
5. sit down

6. some plans need luck
7. check cashing
8. let them make conditions
9. had the
10. both days

3　わたり音（音のスムーズ化）

母音が連続するときは、[j] や [w] のようなわたり音（glide）を間に入れると滑らかに発音できます。[j] は唇を横に引っ張り出す音ですが、同じような唇の形で発音される母音 [i(:)] の後に現れます。一方、[w] は唇を大きく突き出して発音する音ですが、これも同じような唇の形で発音される母音 [u(:)] の後に現れます。ただ、わたり音をあまり強調しすぎるとかえって不自然な発音になるので注意してください。

CD 1-71

Go away.

Go$^{(w)}$away.
Go away.（不自然な発音）

I also need the other one.

I$^{(j)}$also need the$^{(j)}$other one.
I(j)also need the(j)other one.（不自然な発音）

Exercise 3-7　　　　　　　　　　　　　　　　　　　　　　CD 1-72

例にならって、適当な場所にわたり音を入れてみましょう。その後、音声について繰り返し発音してみましょう。

例		
she isn't	→	she$^{(j)}$isn't
who is	→	who$^{(w)}$is

1. go anywhere　→
2. so honest　→
3. through our　→
4. you are　→
5. he is　→
6. do I?　→

7. I asked   →

8. to open   →

9. she always   →

10. too often   →

4 | 混じり合う音（音の同化）

子音の [t], [d], [s], [z] の後に [j] が続くと、2 つの音が融合してそれぞれに似た性質を持つ新しい音に変化します。これを「音の同化」と言います。

Exercise 3-8

音声の後について発音してみましょう。

CD 1-73

1. [t] + [j] = [tʃ]（チ）

What's your name?	[wətʃəʳ **neɪm**]
Can't you do it?	[kæn tʃu: **du:**⁽ʷ⁾ɪt]
actually	[**æk**tʃuli]
Don't you like it?	[doʊn tʃu: **laɪ** kɪt]
Wouldn't you?	[**wʊd**n tʃu:]
Haven't you? No, not yet.	[**hæv**n tʃu: nou nɑ **tʃet**]
I'll let you know.	[aɪl letʃə **noʊ**]
Can I get you a drink?	[k'naɪ getʃu:ə **drɪŋk**]
We thought you weren't coming.	[wi θɑ: tʃu: wəʳːnt **kʌmɪŋ**]
I'll bet you ten bucks he forgot.	[aɪl betʃə **ten** bʌksi: fəʳ**gɑt**]
Is that your final answer?	[ɪz ðætʃəʳ faɪn'**læn** səʳ]
perpetual	[pəʳ**pet**ʃu⁽ʷ⁾əl]
virtual	[**vəʳ**ːtʃu⁽ʷ⁾əl]

CD 1-74

2. [d] + [j] = [dʒ]（ヂ）

Did you see it?	[dɪdʒə **si:**⁽ʲ⁾ɪt]
How did you like it?	[hau dʒə **laɪ** kɪt]
Could you tell?	[kudʒu **tel**]
Where did you send your check?	[weəʳdʒə sendʒəʳ **tʃek**]
What did your family think?	[wədʒəʳ **fæm**li θɪŋk]
Did you find your keys?	[dɪdʒə faɪn dʒəʳ **ki:z**]
We followed your instructions.	[wi faloʊ dʒəʳɪn **strʌk**ʃənz]
education	[edʒu**keɪ**ʃən]

indivi<u>d</u>ual	[ɪndəvɪdʒu^(w)əl]
gra<u>d</u>uation	[grædʒu^(w)eɪʃən]
gra<u>d</u>ual	[**græ**dʒu^(w)əl]

CD 1-75

3. [s] + [j] = [ʃ] （シ）

Ye<u>s, y</u>ou are.	[**je**ʃu ɑəʳ]
Ble<u>ss y</u>ou!	[**ble**ʃu]
Pre<u>ss y</u>our hands together.	[preʃəʳ **hændz** t'geðəʳ]
Can you dre<u>ss y</u>ourself?	[k'nju: **dre**ʃəʳ self]
You can pa<u>ss y</u>our exams thi<u>s y</u>ear.	[juk'n pæʃəʳ ɪgzæmz ðɪʃɪəʳ]
I'll try to gue<u>ss y</u>our age.	[aɪl traɪdə geʃəʳ**eɪdʒ**]
Let him ga<u>s y</u>our car for you.	[ledɪm gæʃəʳ **kɑəʳ** fəʳ ju:]

CD 1-76

4. [z] + [j] = [ʒ] （ジ）

How'<u>s y</u>our family?	[haʊʒəʳ **fæm**li]
How wa<u>s y</u>our trip?	[haʊ wəʒəʳ **trɪp**]
Who'<u>s y</u>our friend?	[hu:ʒəʳ **frend**]
Where'<u>s y</u>our mom?	[weəʳʒəʳ **mɑm**]
When'<u>s y</u>our birthday?	[wenʒəʳ **bəʳ:**θdeɪ]
She say<u>s y</u>ou're OK.	[ʃi seʒəʳoʊ **keɪ**]
Who doe<u>s y</u>our hair?	[hu: dəʒəʳ **heəʳ**]
ca<u>su</u>al	[**kæ**ʒu^(w)əl]
vi<u>su</u>al	[**vɪ**ʒu^(w)əl]

Exercise 3-9 CD 1-77

1. 〜 10. の語句はどのような発音になるでしょう。例にならって発音記号またはカタカナで書いてみてください。その後、音声をよく聞き繰り返し発音してみましょう。

例			
put your	→ [pʊtʃəʳ]	（プッチャ）	
gradual	→ [grædʒu^(w)əl]	（グラヂュアル）	

1. did you	→ [	] （	）
2. who's your	→ [	] （	）
3. just your	→ [	] （	）
4. gesture	→ [	] （	）
5. miss you	→ [	] （	）
6. tissue	→ [	] （	）

7. got your → [   ] (   )

8. where's your → [   ] (   )

9. had your → [   ] (   )

Exercise 3-10

次の文章で 1) 音の連結、2) 音の脱落、3) 音の同化が起こっているところに下線を引いてみましょう。必要があれば、適当な場所にわたり音 [j] [w] も書き入れてください。最初の 2 つの文は例としてすでに下線が入れてあります。

Hello, **my** na<u>me</u> <u>is</u> Ann. I'm taki<u>ng</u> American **Accent** Training. There's a **lot** to learn, but I **hope** to make it as **enjoyable** as possible. I should pick **up** on the American **intonation** pattern pretty **easily**, although the **only** way to **get** it is to **practice** all of the time. I use the **up** and down, or **peaks** and valleys, **intonation** more than I **used** to. I've been paying attention to **pitch, too.** It's like **walking** down a **stair**case. I've been **talking** to a lot of **Americans** lately, and they tell me that I'm **easier** to under**stand.** **Any**way, I could go **on** and on, but the **important** thing is to **listen** well and sound **good. Well,** what do you **think? Do** I?

Exercise 3-11

音声では、音の連結・脱落・同化部分がやや誇張されてゆっくりと話されています。モデルについてスムーズに読めるまで繰り返し練習をしてみましょう。最後は，自然な速さで音の連結を意識しながら文章を読んでみましょう。発音記号に不慣れな人は、Exercise 3-10 の文章の方を使って練習してみてください。

[həloʊ **maɪ** neɪ mɪz æn aɪm teɪkɪŋə merəkə **næk**sen⁽ᵗ⁾treɪnɪŋ ðeəʳ zə **la**tə ləʳːn bə daɪ **hoʊp** t' meɪ kɪ dəzen **dʒɔɪəbləz** pasəbl aɪ ʃʊd pɪ **kʌp**an ði⁽ʲ⁾əmerəkə nɪntəneɪʃ'n pædəʳn prɪdi⁽ʲ⁾**iː**zəli ɑːldoʊ ði⁽ʲ⁾**oʊ**nli weɪdə **ge**dɪdɪz t' **prækt**ɪ saːləv ð' taɪm aɪ⁽ʲ⁾juːz ði⁽ʲ⁾**ʌp**'n daʊn ɔəʳ **piːk** s'n væli zɪntəneɪʃən mɔəʳ ðə naɪ **juːs** tuː aɪvbin peɪɪŋə tenʃən t' **pɪtʃ tuː** ɪtslaɪ **kwaːkɪŋ** daʊ nə **steəʳ**keɪs aɪvbin **taːkɪŋ** tuː⁽ʷ⁾ə ladəvə **merək**ən zleɪtli 'n ðeɪ tel mi ðə daɪ**miːz**ɪəʳ tuː⁽ʷ⁾ʌndəʳ**stænd** enɪweɪ aɪ kʊd goʊ⁽ʷ⁾**ɑ** nə nan bʌ⁽ᵗ⁾ði⁽ʲ⁾ɪm**pɔəʳ**tən⁽ᵗ⁾ θɪŋɪz t' **lɪs**nwelən saʊn⁽ᵈ⁾**gʊd wel** wədju **θɪŋk duː**⁽ʷ⁾aɪ]

みなさんは今の段階でこのような発音する必要はありませんが、ネイティブスピーカーがこのように発音したときに理解できることは大切です。音声の後について実際に発音して確認しましょう。

I have got to go.	→	[aɪv gɑtə **goʊ**]
I have got a book.	→	[aɪv gɑtə **bʊk**]
Do you want to dance?	→	[dju wɑnə **dæns**]
Want a banana?	→	[wɑnə bənænə]
Let me in.	→	[lemi **ɪn**]
Let me go.	→	[lemi **goʊ**]
I'll let you know.	→	[aɪl letʃə **noʊ**]
Did you do it?	→	[dɪdʒə **du:** ɪt]
Not yet.	→	[nɑ **tʃet**]
I'll meet you later.	→	[aɪl mi:tʃu **leɪdər**]
What do you think?	→	[wədju **θɪŋk**]
What did you do with it?	→	[wədʒu: **du:** wɪð ɪt]
How did you like it?	→	[haʊdʒə **laɪk** ɪt]
When did you get it?	→	[wen dʒu **ge**dɪt]
Why did you take it?	→	[hwaɪdʒu **teɪ** kɪt]
Why don't you try it?	→	[hwaɪ (doʊ)n tʃu **traɪ** ɪt]
What are you waiting for?	→	[wədjə **weɪtɪŋ** fɔər]
What are you doing?	→	[wətʃə **du:ɪŋ**]
How is it going?	→	[haʊzɪt **goʊɪŋ**]
Where's the what-you-may-call-it?	→	[weərz ðə **wʌtʃə**meɪkɑ:lɪt]
Where's what-is-his-name?	→	[weərz **wʌt**sɪzneɪm]
How about it?	→	[haʊ ˈbaʊt ɪt]
He has got to hurry because he is late.	→	[hi:z gɑtə **hər:ri** ˈkəz hi:z **leɪt**]
I could've been a contender.	→	[aɪ kʊdə binə kənten**dər**]
Could you speed it up, please?	→	[kʊdʒu: spi: dɪ **dʌp** pli:z]
Would you mind if I tried it?	→	[wʊdʒu: maɪndɪfaɪ **traɪ** dɪt]
Aren't you Bob Barker?	→	[ɑərntʃu: bɑb **bɑərkər**]
Can't you see it my way for a change?	→	[kæntʃu: si: ɪt **maɪ** weɪ fər ə **tʃeɪndʒ**]
Don't you get it?	→	[doʊntʃə **ge**dɪt]
I should have told you.	→	[aɪ ʃʊdə toʊld**ʒu:**]
Tell her (that) I miss her.	→	[telər aɪ **mɪs**ər]
Tell him (that) I miss him.	→	[telɪm aɪ **mɪs**ɪm]

UNIT 4

母音の発音

ここからしばらく母音と子音の練習をしてみましょう。まずは母音からです。「アー」と言いながら「のど仏」を指で触ると振動を感じます。これは「のど仏」の中にある声帯が振動しているためで、このような音を「有声音」と言います。声帯が振動しない音は「無声音」と呼ばれます。母音はすべて有声音です。

1 | Cat? Caught? Cut?（「ア」系列の 3 つの母音）

英語には日本語の「ア」に相当する主な母音が全部で 3 つあります。

1) [ɑ(:)]

日本語で「ア」と言いながら、下あごを下がるところまで下げてください。慣れるまでは不自然と思うぐらい大きく口を開けてみましょう。舌は全体的に低くし、やや後ろ寄りになります。あごを下げると自然に口が開き舌も低くなるので特に意識しなくても構いません。歯医者で診察してもらうときに「アー」と口を開けるときのイメージです。

2) [æ]

アメリカ英語の典型的な響きを作り出す母音の 1 つで、発音記号を見ても分かるように「ア」と「エ」の中間音です。口を大きく開け、舌先を下の前歯の裏側に近づけ、舌を前の方に突き出すような感じで発音してください。発音するときはのどの緊張を伴います。

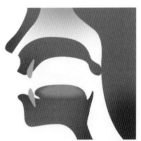

3) [ʌ]/[ə]

口をわずかに開け、あごは下げず、舌の後方で弱く「ア」と発音します。[ʌ] と [ə] の口の構えは同じと考えて構いません。[ʌ] はストレスのある音節に、[ə] はストレスのない音節に現れます。英語の母音は弱くなると [ə] になることが多く、英語では最も頻繁に現れる母音です。「イ」「ウ」「オ」「ア」ともつかないあいまいな音に聞こえるので「あいまい母音」またはシュワ（schwa）と呼ばれています。

音声の後について発音してみましょう。リストは上から下に向かって読まれます。

[æ]	[ɑ(:)]	[ʌ]
Ann	on	un-
ban	bond	bun
can	con	come
cat	caught/cot	cut
Dan	Don/dawn	done
fan	fawn	fun
gap	gone	gun
hat	hot	hut
Jan	John	jump
lamp	lawn	lump
man	monster	Monday
matter	motto	mutter
Nan	non-	none/nun
gnat	not/knot	nut
pan	pawn	pun
ran	Ron	run
sand	sawn	sun
shall	Sean	shut
chance	chalk	chuck
tack	talk	tuck
van	Von	vug
wax	want	won/one
yam	yawn	young
zap	czar	result

Unit 2 でも見たように、that, than, as, at, and, have, had, can は文中では普通弱く発音されます。母音部分のもともとの発音は [æ] ですが、弱く発音されると [ə] に変わります。ナチュラルスピードの英語では音自体が消えてしまうこともあります。音声の後について繰り返し発音してみましょう。

	強く発音されたとき	弱く発音されたとき	例文
that	[ðæt]	[ð't] [ðət]	He said <u>that</u> it's OK.
than	[ðæn]	[ð'n] [ðən]	It's bigger <u>than</u> before.
as	[æz]	['z] [əz]	<u>As</u> soon <u>as</u> he gets here . . .

強く発音されたとき	弱く発音されたとき	例文
at [æt]	['t] [ət]	Look <u>at</u> the time!
and [ænd]	['n] [ən]	ham <u>and</u> eggs
have [hæv]	['v] [həv]	Where <u>have</u> you been?
had [hæd]	['d] [həd]	He <u>had</u> been at home.
can [kæn]	[k'n] [kən]	<u>Can</u> you do it?

Exercise 4-3

次の文章の中には、[æ] が 6 個、[ɑ(ː)] が 10 個、[ə] が約 65 個あります（[ə] は他の母音で発音されることもあるので、数はあくまで目安です）。下線を引いてみましょう（それぞれの最初の音は例としてすでに下線が引いてあります）。

H<u>e</u>llo, **my** name is <u>Ann</u>. I'm taking American **Accent** Training. There's a **lot** to learn, but I **hope** to make it as **enjoyable** as possible. I should pick **up** on the American **intonation** pattern pretty **easily**, although the **only** way to **get** it is to **practice** all of the time. I use the **up** and down, or **peaks** and valleys, **intonation** more than I **used** to. I've been paying attention to **pitch, too**. It's like **walking** down a **stair**case. I've been **talking** to a lot of **Americans** lately, and they tell me that I'm **easier** to unde**rstand**. Anyway, I could go **on** and on, but the **important** thing is to **listen** well and sound **good**. **Well**, what do you **think**? **Do** I?

Exercise 4-4

CD 1-82

[æ] を集中的に練習します。下線部に注意しながら、音声の後について繰り返し発音してみましょう。

The T<u>a</u>n M<u>a</u>n

A f<u>a</u>shionably t<u>a</u>n m<u>a</u>n s<u>a</u>t casually at b<u>a</u>t st<u>a</u>nd, l<u>a</u>shing a h<u>a</u>ndful of pr<u>a</u>ctice b<u>a</u>ts. The m<u>a</u>nager, a cr<u>a</u>bby old b<u>a</u>g of bones, p<u>a</u>ssed by and l<u>a</u>ughed, "You're about <u>a</u>verage, Jack. C<u>a</u>n't you l<u>a</u>sh f<u>a</u>ster than th<u>a</u>t?" Jack had h<u>a</u>d enough, so he cl<u>a</u>mbered to his feet and l<u>a</u>shed b<u>a</u>ts f<u>a</u>ster than any m<u>a</u>n had ever l<u>a</u>shed b<u>a</u>ts. As a m<u>a</u>tter of f<u>a</u>ct, he l<u>a</u>shed b<u>a</u>ts so f<u>a</u>st that he seemed to d<u>a</u>nce. The m<u>a</u>nager was agh<u>a</u>st. "Jack, you're a m<u>a</u>ster b<u>a</u>t l<u>a</u>sher!" he g<u>a</u>sped. S<u>a</u>tisfied at l<u>a</u>st, Jack s<u>a</u>t b<u>a</u>ck and never l<u>a</u>shed another b<u>a</u>t.

[ɑ(ː)] を集中的に練習します。下線部に注意しながら音声の後について繰り返し発音してみましょう。

A Lot of Long, Hot Walks in the Garden

John was not sorry when the boss called off the walks in the garden. Obviously, to him, it was awfully hot, and the walks were far too long. He had not thought that walking would have caught on the way it did, and he fought the policy from the onset. At first, he thought he could talk it over at the law office and have it quashed, but a small obstacle halted that thought. The top lawyers always bought coffee at the shop across the lawn and they didn't want to stop on John's account. John's problem was not office politics, but office policy. He resolved the problem by bombing the garden.

[ʌ] と [ə] を集中的に練習します。下線部に注意しながら音声の後について繰り返し発音してみましょう。

What Must the Sun Above Wonder About?

Some pundits proposed that the sun wonders unnecessarily about sundry and assorted conundrums. One cannot but speculate what can come of their proposal. It wasn't enough to trouble us, but it was done so underhandedly that hundreds of sun lovers rushed to the defense of their beloved sun. None of this was relevant on Monday, however, when the sun burned up the entire country.

2 | Beat? Bit? (「イ」「ウ」系列の母音)

次は日本語の「イ」「ウ」に相当する英語の母音です。それぞれ 2 種類あります。まずは「イ」系の母音から見てみましょう。

2-1 | 「イ」系列の母音

1) [iː]

日本語の「イ」よりも唇を大きく左右に引っ張ってください。舌の前方が口の天井に向けて高くなりますが、これも唇をしっかり横に引っ張ることで自然にできるようになります。発音するときには口の緊張を伴います。

2) [ɪ]

[iː] ほど唇を横に引っ張る必要はなく、「イ」と「エ」の中間音のような母音です。口の緊張は伴いません。

2つは長さだけの違いのように聞こえるかもしれませんが、そうではありません。あくまで別々の母音であることを意識して練習しましょう。

[i:] と [ɪ] の発音練習です。音声の後について繰り返し発音してみましょう。

[i:]	[ɪ]	
1. eat	it	I **eat** it.
2. beat	bit	The **beat** is a bit strong.
3. keys	kiss	Give me a **kiss** for the **keys**.
4. cheek	chick	The chick's **cheek** is soft.
5. deed	did	He **did** the **deed**.
6. feet	fit	These **shoes** fit my **feet**.
7. feel	fill	Do you feel that we should **fill** it?
8. green	grin	The Martian's **grin** was **green**.
9. heat	hit	Last **summer**, the **heat** hit **hard**.
10. heel	hill	Put your **heel** on the **hill**.
11. jeep	Jill	Jill's **jeep** is here.
12. creep	crypt	Let's **creep** near the **crypt**.
13. leap	lip	He bumped his **lip** when he **leaped**.
14. meal	mill	She had a **meal** at the **mill**.
15. neat	knit	He can **knit neatly**.
16. peel	pill	Don't **peel** that **pill**!
17. reed	rid	Get rid of that **reed**.
18. seek	sick	We seek the **sixth** sick sheik's **sheep**.
19. sheep	ship	There are **sheep** on the **ship**.
20. sleep	slip	The girl **sleeps** in a **slip**.
21. steal	still	He still **steals**.
22. Streep	strip	Meryl **Streep** is in a **comic** strip.
23. team	Tim	**Tim** is on the **team**.
24. these	this	**These** are better than **this** one.
25. thief	thing	The **thief** took my **thing**.
26. weep	whip	Who **weeps** from the **whips**?

1) 最初の単語は [iː]、2番目の単語は [ɪ] を含んでいます。音声の後について繰り返し発音してみましょう。

eat / it   sheep / ship   seat / sit   neat / nit   feet / fit   sleep / slip

2) [iː] は太字にして、[ɪ] は下線を引いてあります（母音に [r] が続く場合は Unit 7 を参照）。CD の後について繰り返し発音してみましょう。

Pick a Peak

People who p_i_ck p**ea**ks w**ee**kly s**ee**m to n**ee**d to app_ea_r d**ee**p _i_n order to b**e** d_i_st_i_ngu_i_shed from m_e_re p**ea** p_i_ckers. P**e**ter, a champ_i_on p**ea**k p_i_cker, thought he'd b**e e**ven n**ea**ter _i_f he were the d**ee**pest p**ea**k p_i_cker _i_n P**eo**ria, Ph**oe**n_i_x, and New Z**ea**land. On h_i_s p**ea**k p**ea**k p_i_cking w**ee**k, though, P**e**ter, a p**ea**k p_i_cker's p**ea**k p_i_cker, r**ea**lized that he was not d**ee**p. Th_i_s _i_s not **ea**sy for a p**ea**k p_i_cker to adm_i_t and _i_t p_i_tched P**e**ter _i_nto a p_i_t of p**ea**k p_i_cking despair. H**e** was p_i_tiful for thr**ee** w**ee**ks and then l_i_fted h_i_mself to h_i_therto unrev**ea**led personal p**ea**ks.

2-2 「ウ」系列の母音

1) [uː]

日本語の「ウ」よりも唇をかなり強く丸めてください。舌の後方が口の天井に向かって盛り上がりますが、唇を丸めれば自然に後舌は盛り上がります。発音するときには口の緊張を伴います。

2) [ʊ]

[uː] ほど唇を丸める必要はなく、「ウ」と「オ」の中間音のような母音です。口の緊張は伴いません。

[iː] と [ɪ] のときのように、[uː] と [ʊ] も単なる長さの違いではありません。あくまで別々の母音であると意識しましょう。

[uː] と [ʊ] の発音練習です。音声の後について繰り返し発音してみましょう。

[uː]	[ʊ]
1. booed	book
2. boo	bushel
3. cooed	could
4. cool	cushion
5. food	foot

[uː]		[ʊ]
6.	fool	full
7.	gooed	good
8.	who'd	hood
9.	kook	cook
10.	crew	crook
11.	Luke	look
12.	nuke	nook
13.	pool	pull
14.	pooch	put
15.	shoe	sugar
16.	suit	soot
17.	shoot	should
18.	stewed	stood
19.	toucan	took
20.	wooed	would

Exercise 4-10

次の文章の中には、[ʊ] が 3 個、[uː] が 7 個あります。下線を引いてみましょう（それぞれの最初の音は例としてすでに下線が引いてあります）。

Hello, **my** name is Ann. I'm taking American **Accent** Training. There's a **lot** to learn, but I **hope** to make it as **enjoyable** as possible. I sho̲uld pick **up** on the American **intonation** pattern pretty **easily**, although the **only** way to **get** it is to **practice** all of the time. I u̲se the **up** and down, or **peaks** and valleys, **intonation** more than I **used** to. I've been paying attention to **pitch, too**. It's like **walking** down a **stair**case. I've been **talking** to a lot of **Americans** lately, and they tell me that I'm **easier** to unde**rstand**. Any**way, I could go **on** and on, but the **important** thing is to **listen** well and sound **good**. **Well**, what do you **think? Do** I?

Exercise 4-11   CD 2-2

[ʊ] を含む早口ことばです。どれくらい早く言えるかチャレンジしてみましょう。

How much wood	[haʊ mʌtʃ wʊd]
would a woodchuck chuck,	[wʊdə wʊdtʃʌk tʃʌk]
if a woodchuck	[ɪfə wʊdtʃʌk]
could chuck	[kʊd tʃʌk]
wood?	[wʊd]

How many cookies	[haʊ meni kʊkiz]
could a good cook cook,	[kʊdə gʊd kʊk kʊk]
if a good cook	[ɪfə gʊd kʊk]
could cook	[kʊd kʊk]
cookies?	[kʊkiz]

次は [u:] を集中的に練習します。下線部に注意しながら音声の後について繰り返し発音してみましょう。

A true fool will choose to drool in a pool to stay cool. Who knew that such fools were in the schools used tools, and flew balloons? Lou knew and now you do, too.

次は [ʊ] を集中的に練習します。下線部に注意しながら音声の後について繰り返し発音してみましょう。

Booker Woolsey was a good cook. One day, he took a good look at his full schedule and decided that he could write a good cookbook. He knew that he could, and thought that he should, but he wasn't sure that he ever would. Once he had made up his mind, he stood up, pulled up a table, took a cushion, and put it on a bushel basket of sugar in the kitchen nook. He shook out his writing hand and put his mind to creating a good, good cookbook.

2-3 母音の長さ

[i:] と [ɪ]、[u:] と [ʊ] は単なる長さの違いではないことを強調しました。発音するときに口を緊張させる [i:] と [u:] は、そうでない [ɪ] や [ʊ] に比べると本質的に長くなります。しかし、英単語内に出てくる母音の長さを決めるのはその後に続く子音です。後に来る子音が無声（＝声帯が振動していない）のときの方が有声（＝声帯が振動している）のときよりも短くなります。実際に聞き比べてみましょう。

CD 2-5

| beat | [bi:t] | bead | [bi::d] |
| bit | [bɪt] | bid | [bɪ:d] |

[i:] も [ɪ] も、最後の子音が無声の [t] のときの方が有声の [d] のときよりも短くなっているのが分かるでしょう。これは [t] と [d] に限ったことではなく、後にどんな子音が続いても同じことが言えます。

音声の後について発音してみましょう。まず、各列を上から下に向かって練習し，その後、各ペアごとに、最後は左から右に向かって発音してください。特に母音の長さに注意してみましょう。

	[iː]				[ɪ]	
1.	beat	bead	·	bit	bid
2.	seat	seed	·	sit	Sid
3.	heat	he'd	·	hit	hid
4.	Pete	impede	·	pit	rapid
5.	feet	feed	·	fit	fin
6.	niece	knees	·	miss	Ms.
7.	geese	he's	·	hiss	his
8.	deep	deed	·	disk	did
9.	neat	need	·	knit	(nid)
10.	leaf	leave	·	lift	live

3 | Bet? Bait? (長母音と短母音)

最後はここまで練習してきた母音も復習しながら、長母音と短母音の練習をしてみましょう。ここでは二重母音も長母音の仲間に入れています。

＊ [æ] は一般に短母音に分類されますが，実際は長めに発音されることが多いため、ここでは長母音として扱っています。

まずは長母音の練習です。音声の後について発音してみましょう。どの列も左から右に向かって読まれています。

	[æ]	[aʊ]	[ɑ(ː)]	[aɪ]	[eɪ]	[iː]	[uː]	[oʊ]
1.	at	out	ought	I'd	ate	eat	ooze	own
2.	bat	about	bought	bite	bait	beat	boot	boat
3.	cat	couch	caught	kite	cane	keys	cool	coat
4.	chat	chowder	chalk	child	change	cheek	choose	chose
5.	dad	doubt	dot	dial	date	deed	do	don't
6.	fat	found	fought	fight	fate	feet	food	phone
7.	fallow	fountain	fall	file	fail	feel	fool	foal
8.	gas	gown	got	kite	gate	geese	ghoul	go

[æ]	[aʊ]	[ɑ(:)]	[aɪ]	[eɪ]	[i:]	[u:]	[oʊ]
9. hat	how	hot	height	hate	heat	hoot	hope
10. Hal	howl	hall	heil	hail	heel	who'll	hole
11. Jack	jowl	jock	giant	jail	jeep	jewel	Joel
12. crab	crowd	crawl	crime	crate	creep	cruel	crow
13. last	loud	lost	line	late	Lee	Lou	low
14. mat	mountain	mop	might	mate	mean	moon	moan
15. gnat	now	not	night	Nate	neat	noon	note
16. pal	pound	Paul	pile	pail	peel	pool	pole
17. rat	round	rot	right	rate	real	rule	role
18. sat	sound	soft	sight	sale	seal	Sue	soul
19. shall	shower	shawl	shine	shade	she	shoe	show
20. slap	slouch	slop	slide	slade	sleep	slew	slow
21. stag	stout	stop	style	stale	steal	stool	stole
22. strap	Stroud	straw	stride	straight	stream	strew	stroll
23. tap	town	top	type	tape	team	tool	told
24. that	thou	thar	thine	they	these		though
25. thang	thousand	thought	thigh	thane	thief		throw
26. van	vow	volume	viper	vain	veal	voodoo	vote
27. wax	Wow!	wash	wipe	wane	wheel	woo	woe
28. yank	Yow!	yawn	yikes	Yale	yield	you	yo
29. zap	Zowie!	zombie	xylophone	zany	zebra	zoo	Zoe

Exercise 4-16

次の文章に含まれる長母音に下線を引いてみましょう。[eɪ] が 12 個、[i:]/[i] が 15 個、[æ] は 6 個（これはすでに Exercise 4-3 でやりました）、[aʊ] は 3 個あります。

Hello, my name is Ann. I'm taking American **Accent** Training. There's a **lot** to learn, but I **hope** to make it as **enjoyable** as possible. I should pick **up** on the American **intonation** pattern pretty **easily**, although the **only** way to **get** it is to **practice** all of the time. I use the **up** and down, or **peaks** and valleys, **intonation** more than I **used** to. I've been paying attention to **pitch, too.** It's like **walking** down a **stair**case. I've been **talking** to a lot of **Americans** lately, and they tell me that I'm **easier** to under**stand.** **Anyway,** I could go **on** and on, but the **important** thing is to **listen** well and sound **good. Well,** what do you **think? Do** I?

次は短母音の練習です。[e] は日本語の「エ」で代用して問題ありません。[ɚ] はアメリカ英語特有の母音で [r] の音色を持った [ə] です。２つの記号を使っていますが、あくまで１つの音で、[ə] の口の構えでそり舌にして発音します（詳しくは Unit 7 を参照）。辞書によっては [ɚ] と表記してあるものもありますが、本書では分かりやすさを考え、[ɚʳ] と表記します。音声の後について発音してみましょう。

[e]	[ɪ]	[ʊ]	[ə]	[ɚʳ(ː)]
1. end	it		un-	earn
2. bet	bit	book	but	burn
3. kept	kid	could	cut	curt
4. check	chick		chuck	church
5. debt	did		does	dirt
6. fence	fit	foot	fun	first
7. fell	fill	full		furl
8. get	guilt	good	gut	girl
9. help	hit	hook	hut	hurt
10. held	hill	hood	hull	hurl
11. gel	Jill		jump	jerk
12. ked	kid	cook	cud	curd
13. crest	crypt	crook	crumb	
14. let	little	look	lump	lurk
15. men	milk		muck	murmur
16. net	knit	nook	nut	nerd
17. pet	pit	put	putt	pert
18. pell	pill	pull		pearl
19. red	rid	root	rut	rural
20. said	sit	soot	such	search
21. shed	shin	should	shut	sure
22. sled	slim		slug	slur
23. stead	still	stood	stuff	stir
24.	It'd stick.	It stood.	It's done.	It's dirt.
25. stretch	string		struck	
26. tell	tip	took	ton	turn
27. then	this		thus	
28.	thing		thug	third
29. vex	vim		vug	verb

母音の発音 **63**

次の文章の中に含まれる短母音に下線を引いてみましょう。[e] が約 12 個、[ɪ] は 9 〜 24 個あります（ストレスのない音節ではこれらの母音は弱くなり [ə] と発音されることもあるので、数はあくまで目安です）。

Hello, **my** name is Ann. I'm taking American **Accent** Training. There's a **lot** to learn, but I **hope** to make it as **enjoyable** as possible. I should pick **up** on the American **intonation** pattern pretty **easily**, although the **only** way to **get** it is to **practice** all of the time. I use the **up** and down, or **peaks** and valleys, **intonation** more than I **used** to. I've been paying attention to **pitch, too**. It's like **walking** down a **stair**case. I've been **talking** to a lot of **Americans** lately, and they tell me that I'm **easier** to under**stand**. **Any**way, I could go **on** and on, but the **important** thing is to **listen** well and sound **good**. **Well**, what do you **think**? **Do** I?

最後は [eɪ], [æ], [e] を集中的に練習します。音声の後について繰り返し発音してみましょう。

1) late / lack / let   take / tack / tech   mate / mat / met
    hail / Hal / hell   fate / fat / fetch   cane / can / Ken

2)   Take a High-Tech Tack

Say, Ray, take a tack. A high-tack tack? No, Ray, a high-tech tack, eight high-tech tacks, take them. Then find a way to make a place for the tacks on the day bed. Hey, you lay the tacks on the paper place mat on the table, not on the day bed, Ray. At your age, why do you always make the same mistakes?

UNIT 5

Ｔの発音

次は子音の練習です。まずはＴの音から見てみましょう。

発音方法
舌先を上の歯の後ろ（＝歯茎）につけ、一度完全に息の流れを止めた後、一気に吐き出します（＝息を破裂させる）。

これがＴの最も標準的な発音 [t] です。[t] の口の構えのまま声帯を振動させると（＝有声化すると）[d] になります。[t] は単語内のどの位置に現れるかによって少しずつ発音が変わります。

1 語頭のＴ

ストレス音節で始まる単語では、語頭のＴは普通の [t] よりもかなり強く息を吐き出して（＝破裂させて）発音します。（以下、[tʰ] と表記します）

        teach   [tʰiːtʃ]   tooth   [tʰuːθ]

厳密に言うと鍵を握るのはＴを含む音節にストレスがあるかどうかです。語中でもストレス音節の始めに来るとＴは [tʰ] となります。

        atomic   [ə•tʰám•ɪk]   pretend   [prɪ•tʰénd]

Exercise 5-1   CD 2-10

Ｔを [t] または [tʰ] と発音する練習をします。音声の後について繰り返し発音してみましょう。

1. It took Tim ten times to try the telephone.
2. Stop touching Ted's toes.
3. Turn toward Stella and study her contract together.
4. Control your tears.
5. It's Tommy's turn to tell the teacher the truth.

2 語中の T

T の前に母音があり、その後にストレスのない母音が来るときは [d] のような音になることがあります。この音変化はアメリカ英語ではとてもよく見られるのでこの後十分に練習しましょう。厳密には日本語のラ行の出だしの子音に近い音で、私たち日本人にとっては逆に発音しやすいかもしれません。water は「ワダー」や「ワラー」のように聞こえます。この変化は単語間でも起こります。

butter	[bʌdəʳ]	a lot of	[ə ladəv]
water	[wɑdəʳ]	put it in	[pʊdɪ dɪn]

Exercise 5-2   CD 2-11

まず Betty bought a bit of better butter. を [bedi badə bɪdə bedəʳ bʌdəʳ]（ベディ・バダ・ビダ・ベダ・バダ）と何度かゆっくり発音してみてください。その後、次の文章を音声の後について繰り返してください。

Betty Bought a Bit of Better Butter

Betty bought a bit of better butter,	[bedi badə bɪdə bedəʳ bʌdəʳ]
But, said she,	[bʌ⁽ᵗ⁾sed ʃi]
This butter's bitter.	[ðɪs bʌdəʳz bɪdəʳ]
If I put it in my batter,	[ɪf aɪ pʊdi dɪn maɪ bædəʳ]
It'll make my batter bitter.	[ɪtl meɪk maɪ bædəʳ bɪdəʳ]

Exercise 5-3   CD 2-12

T を [d] のように発音する練習を続けます。音声の後について繰り返し発音してみましょう。

＊ 母音と母音の間だけでなく、母音と [n], [r], [l] に挟まれたときもこの音変化が起こるときがあります。

Betty bought a bit of better butter.	[bedi badə bɪdə bedəʳ bʌdəʳ]
Pat ought to sit on a lap.	[pædɑːdə sɪdanə læp]

1. What a good **idea**.   [wədə gʊdaɪ diː⁽ʲ⁾ə]
2. Put it in a **bottle**.   [pʊdɪdɪnə bɑdl]
3. Write it in a **letter**.   [raɪdɪdɪnə ledəʳ]
4. Set it on the metal **gutter**.   [sedɪdan ðə medl gʌdəʳ]
5. Put all the **data** in the **computer**.   [pʊdɑːl ðə deɪdə ɪn ðə kʼmpjuːdəʳ]
6. Insert a **quarter** in the **meter**.   [ɪnseʳːdə kwɔəʳdəʳ ɪn ðə miːdəʳ]

7. Ge_t a be_tt_er **wa_t_er** hea_t_er. [gedə bedəʳ **wɑdəʳ** hi:dəʳ]

8. Le_t her pu_t a **sweater** on. [ledəʳ pʊdə **swedəʳ** ɑn]

9. **Be_tt_y**'s a_t a **mee_t_ing**. [**bediz** ədə **mi:dɪŋ**]

10. It's ge_tt_ing ho_tt_er and **ho_tt_er**. [ɪts gedɪŋ hadəʳən **hadəʳ**]

11. **Pa_tt_y** ough_t _to write a be_tt_er **le_tt_er**. [**pædi**⁽ʲ⁾ɑːdə raɪd ə bedəʳ **ledəʳ**]

12. **Freida** had a **li_tt_le** me_t_al **bo_tt_le**. [**fri:**də hædə lɪdl medl **bɑdl**]

T が単語の境界で母音に挟まれたときも同じように [d] のような音になります。また、[t] の後に [j] が続くと、Unit 3 で見たように [tʃ] に変化します。音声には What a から That I までの音声しか入っていませんが、それ以外の語句についても発音記号を参考にしながら、繰り返し練習をしてみてください。

	What	**But**	**That**
a	[wədə]	[bədə]	[ðədə]
I	[wədaɪ]	[bədaɪ]	[ðədaɪ]
I'm	[wədaɪm]	[bədaɪm]	[ðədaɪm]
I've	[wədaɪv]	[bədaɪv]	[ðədaɪv]
if	[wədɪf]	[bədɪf]	[ðədɪf]
it	[wədɪt]	[bədɪt]	[ðədɪt]
it's	[wədɪts]	[bədɪts]	[ðədɪts]
is	[wədɪz]	[bədɪz]	[ðədɪz]
isn't	[wədɪzn⁽ᵗ⁾]	[bədɪzn⁽ᵗ⁾]	[ðədɪzn⁽ᵗ⁾]
are	[wədəʳ]	[bədəʳ]	[ðədəʳ]
aren't	[wədɑəʳn⁽ᵗ⁾]	[bədɑəʳn⁽ᵗ⁾]	[ðədɑəʳn⁽ᵗ⁾]
he	[wədi:]	[bədi:]	[ðədi:]
he's	[wədi:z]	[bədi:z]	[ðədi:z]
her	[wədəʳ]	[bədəʳ]	[ðədəʳ]
you	[wətʃu:]	[bətʃu:]	[ðətʃu:]
you'll	[wətʃul]	[bətʃul]	[ðətʃul]
you've	[wətʃu:v]	[bətʃu:v]	[ðətʃu:v]
you're	[wətʃəʳ]	[bətʃəʳ]	[ðətʃəʳ]

3　語末の T

T が語末に来ると息を破裂させない [t] になることがあります（これは [t] の有声音 [d] だけでなく、同じく息を破裂させて発音する [p]/[b], [k]/[g] にも当てはまります）。日本語の詰まる音「ッ」で単語を終えるような感じです。cut であれば「カット」ではなく「カッ」のイメージです。（以下 [⁽ᵗ⁾] と表記します）

combat　　[kɑmbæ⁽ᵗ⁾]　　　　threat　　[θre⁽ᵗ⁾]

meat　　　[miː⁽ᵗ⁾]　　　　　defeat　　[dɪfiː⁽ᵗ⁾]

Exercise 5-5　　　　　　　　　　　　　　　　　　　　　　CD 2-14

単語の最後に来る T の練習です。音声の後について繰り返し発音してみましょう。

1. She hit the hot **hut** with her **hat**.
2. We went to that **Net** site to get what we **needed**.
3. **Pat** was quite **right**, **wasn't** she?
4. **What**? Put my **hat** back!
5. hot, late, fat, goat, hit, put, not, hurt, what, set, paint, wait, sit, dirt, note, fit, lot, light, suit, point, incident, tight

---

4　Cotton の発音

次はストレスのある音節の後に [t] と [n] が続くときの発音です。実はこの 2 つを発音するときの口の構えはほぼ同じです。両方とも舌先を歯茎につけ、息の流れを一度せき止めます。違いは、[t] はそのまま舌を放して口から息を出すのに対し、[n] は舌をつけたまま鼻から息を出し続けるところです。[t] と [n] を連続で発音するときは、[t] の口の構えを作り、その直後に鼻から息を出しながら「ン」と発音します。このときに [t] と [n] の間に母音を入れないよう注意しましょう。cotton が「カット<u>ン</u>」になってはいけません。

written　　[rɪtn]　　　　　sentence　　[sentns]

forgotten　[fəʳgɑtn]　　　certain　　　[səʳːtn]

音声の後について繰り返してみましょう。

1. He's **forgotten** the **carton** of sa<u>t</u>in **mit<u>t</u>ens**.
2. She's **certain** that he has **written** it.
3. The co<u>tt</u>on **curtain** is no<u>t</u> in the **fountain**.
4. The **hikers** wen<u>t</u> in the **mountains**.
5. **Martin** has go<u>tt</u>en a **kitten**.
6. **Stu<u>d</u>ents** study **Latin** in **Britain**.
7. **Whi<u>t</u>ney** has a **patent** on those **sentences**.
8. He has not **forgotten** what was **written** about the **mutant** on the **mountain**.
9. It's not **certain** that it was go<u>tt</u>en from the **fountain**.
10. You need to pu<u>t</u> an **orange** co<u>tt</u>on **curtain** on that **window**.
11. We like that certain **satin** better than the **carton** of co<u>tt</u>on **curtains**.
12. The intercon<u>t</u>inental **hotel** is in **Seattle**.
13. The frigh<u>t</u>ened **witness** had forgo<u>tt</u>en the **important** wri<u>tt</u>en **message**.
14. The child wasn't **beaten** because he had **bitten** the **button**.

[t] と [l] が続く場合

[t] の後に [l] が続く場合も簡単に見てみましょう。この２つの音の口の構えも似ています。違いは [l] では舌先は歯茎についたままなのに、息が舌の両側から流れ続けているところです。一度 [t] の口の構えを作り、その後すぐに舌の両側を下げ、そこから息を出します。

recently	[riːsəntli]	lately	[leɪtli]
partly	[pɑəˈrtli]	frequently	[friːkwəntli]

5　消えるT

Tが [n] とストレスのない母音に挟まれると [n] の影響で [n] 化してまるでTが消えた
ような発音になることがあります。これもアメリカ英語独特の発音です。

Exercise 5-7　　　　　　　　　　　　　　　　　　　　　　　　　CD 2-16

まず単語レベルの練習です。音声の後について繰り返して発音してみましょう。

1. **in**terview　　　　　[ɪnəʳvjuː]
2. **in**terface　　　　　[ɪnəʳfeɪs]
3. **in**terstate　　　　　[ɪnəʳsteɪt]
4. inter**rupt**　　　　　[ɪnəʳrʌpt]
5. inter**fere**　　　　　[ɪnəʳfɪəʳ]
6. inter**active**　　　　[ɪnəʳæktɪv]
7. inter**national**　　　[ɪnəʳnæʃənəl]
8. ad**van**tage　　　　[ədvæn'dʒ]
9. per**cen**tage　　　　[pəʳsen'dʒ]
10. **twen**ty　　　　　[tweni]

Exercise 5-8　　　　　　　　　　　　　　　　　　　　　　　　　CD 2-17

次は文レベルでの練習です。音声の後について繰り返して発音してみましょう。

1. He had a great **in**terview.　　　　　[hi hædə greɪ tɪnəʳvjuː]
2. Try to en**ter** the infor**ma**tion.　　　[traɪdə enəʳ ði ɪnfəʳmeɪʃən]
3. Turn the **print**er on.　　　　　　　[təʳːn ðə prɪnəʳɑn]
4. Finish the **print**ing.　　　　　　　[f'n'ʃ ðə prɪnɪŋ]
5. She's at the inter**national** cen**ter**.　[ʃiːz'⁽ᵗ⁾ði⁽ʲ⁾ɪnəʳnæʃənəl senəʳ]
6. It's twenty de**grees** in Toron**to**.　　[ɪts tweni d'griːzɪn tərɑnoʊ]
7. I don't under**stand** it.　　　　　　[aɪ doʊ nəndəʳstæn d't]
8. She in**vent**ed it in Santa **Mo**nica.　[ʃi⁽ʲ⁾ɪnvent'dɪn sænə mɑnɪkə]
9. He can't even **do** it.　　　　　　　[hi kæniːvən duː⁽ʷ⁾'t]
10. They don't even **want** it.　　　　　[ðeɪ doʊ niːvən wɑn't]
11. They won't ever **try**.　　　　　　[ðeɪ woʊ nevəʳ traɪ]
12. What's the **point** of it?　　　　　[w'ts ðə pɔɪ n'v't]
13. She's the inter**continental** repre**sen**tative. [ʃiz ði⁽ʲ⁾ɪnəʳkɑn⁽ᵗ⁾'nenl repr'zen'd'v]
14. **Hasn't** he?　　　　　　　　　　[hæz niː]
15. **Isn't** he?　　　　　　　　　　　[ɪz niː]

16. **Aren'<u>t</u> I?**   [aə^r naɪ]

17. **Won'<u>t</u> he?**   [woʊ niː]

18. **Doesn'<u>t</u> he?**   [dʌz niː]

19. **Wouldn'<u>t</u> it?**   [wʊd nɪt]

20. **Didn'<u>t</u> I?**   [dɪdn naɪ]

---

6 まとめ

ここまで練習してきたいろいろなＴ音のおさらいです。音声の後について繰り返し発音してみましょう。

1. I don't know what it **means**.   [aɪ doʊn^(t)noʊ wədɪt **miːnz**]

2. But it **looks** like what I **need**.   [bədɪ^(t)lʊk slaɪ kwədaɪ **niːd**]

3. But you **said** that you **wouldn't**.   [bətʃuː **sed** ðətʃuː **wʊd**nt]

4. I **know** what you **think**.   [aɪ **noʊ** wətʃuː **θɪŋk**]

5. But I don't **think** that he **will**.   [bədaɪ doʊn^(t)**θɪŋk** ðədiː **wɪl**]

6. He said that if we can **do** it, he'll **help**.   [hi sed ðə dɪf wi kˀn **duː**^(w)ɪt hil **help**]

7. But isn't it **easier** this way?   [bədɪznɪ **tiː**zɪə^r ðɪ sweɪ]

8. We **want** something that isn't **here**.   [wi **wɑnt** sʌmθɪŋ ðədɪzn^(t) **hɪə^r**]

9. You'll **like** it, but you'll **regret** it later.   [jul **laɪ** kɪt bətʃul rˀ**gre** dɪt **leɪdə^r**]

10. But he's not **right** for what I **want**.   [bədiːz nɑt **raɪt** fə^r wədaɪ **wɑnt**]

11. It's **amazing** what you've **accomplished**.   [ɪts ə**meɪ**zɪŋ wətʃuːvə**kɑm**plɪʃt]

12. What if he **forgets**?   [wədɪfiː fə^r**gets**]

13. OK, but aren't you **missing** something?   [oʊkeɪ bədaə^rntʃuː **mɪ**sɪŋ sʌmθɪŋ]

14. I think that he's OK now.   [aɪ θɪŋk ðədiːz oʊkeɪ naʊ]

15. She **wanted** to, but her **car** broke down.   [ʃi **wɑn**^(t)əd tu: bədə^r **kɑə^r** broʊk daʊn]

16. We **think** that you're taking a **chance**.   [wi **θɪŋk** ðətʃə^r teɪkɪŋə **tʃæns**]

17. They don't know what it's **about**.   [ðeɪ doʊn^(t)noʊ wədɪtsə**baʊt**]

英語では母音の後に [t] が続くと、[d] のときよりも長さが短くなります（Unit 4 の「2-3. 母音の長さ」を参照）。③で見たように語末の [t] や [d] は事実上消えてしまうので、母音の長短が単語を区別する鍵になります。音声をよく聞き、その後について繰り返し発音してみましょう。リストは各グループとも左から右に向かって読まれています。

H			C		
ha!	hod	hot	caw	cod	cot/caught
har	hard	heart	car	card	cart
hall	halled	halt	call	called	
her	heard	hurt	cur	curd	curt
hole	hold	holt	coal	cold	colt
hoe	hoed		co-	code	coat

Exercise 5-11

次の文章で、[d] と発音される T（9 〜 12 個）に（　　）を、息を吐き出さない T（8 個）に下線を記入してください。それぞれ 1 個目は例が記入してあります。

Hello, **my** name is Ann. I'm taking American **Accen**_t_ Training. There's a **lot** to learn, bu(t) I **hope** to make it as **enjoyable** as possible. I should pick **up** on the American **intonation** pattern pretty **easily**, although the **only** way to **get** it is to **practice** all of the time. I use the **up** and down, or **peaks** and valleys, **intonation** more than I **used** to. I've been paying attention to **pitch**, **too**. It's like **walking** down a **stair**case. I've been **talking** to a lot of **Americans** lately, and they tell me that I'm **easier** to under**stand**. **Any**way, I could go **on** and on, but the **important** thing is to **listen** well and sound **good**. **Well**, what do you **think**? **Do** I?

UNIT 6

L の発音

---

1 | L の発音

発音方法

舌先を歯茎（上の歯の裏でも構いません）につけたまま、あごを少し開きぎみにして「ウー」と声を出します。このとき、舌の両側は下がり、そこから息が出続けています。

口の構えは Unit 5 に出てきた [t]/[d], [n] とほぼ同じですが、舌の両側から息を出すところがポイントです。それぞれの音の息の出し方を確認してください。

[t]/[d]
息は舌先を歯茎（＝上の歯の後ろ）から放したとき、そこから一気に外に出ます。

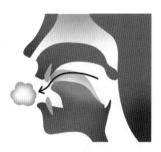

[n]
息は鼻を通って外に出ます。

[l]
息は舌の両側を通り抜け外に出ます。

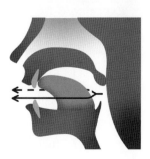

[l] を [t]/[d], [n] と比べながら単語の発音練習をしてみます。最初は上から下に向かって、次は左から右に向かって（3. は左から右だけ）、音声の後について繰り返し発音してみましょう。

1. 語頭

law	gnaw	taw	daw
low	know	toe	dough
lee	knee	tea	D

2. 語中

belly	Benny	Betty
caller	Conner	cotter
alley	Annie's	at ease

3. 語末

A	hole	hold	hone	hoed
	call	called	con	cod
B	fill	full	fool	fail
	fell	feel	fuel	furl

語末に出てくる [l] の練習をしましょう。[l] の前にあいまい母音の [ə] を入れる気持ちで発音すると英語らしくなります。音声では、[l] の正しい舌の位置を意識してもらうため、後ろにも [ə] をつけ、誇張した発音になっています。音声の後について繰り返し発音してみましょう。

1. fill	[fɪələ]		2. full	[fʊələ]
3. fool	[fuː⁽ʷ⁾ələ]		4. fail	[feɪ⁽ʲ⁾ələ]
5. fell	[feələ]		6. feel	[fiː⁽ʲ⁾ələ]
7. fuel	[fjuː⁽ʷ⁾ələ]		8. furl	[fəʳːələ]

次は最後の [ə] を取り [l] を長く伸ばして発音してみましょう。

1. fill	[fɪəllll]		2. full	[fʊəllll]
3. fool	[fuː⁽ʷ⁾əllll]		4. fail	[feɪ⁽ʲ⁾əllll]
5. fell	[feəllll]		6. feel	[fiː⁽ʲ⁾əllll]
7. fuel	[fjuː⁽ʷ⁾əllll]		8. furl	[fəʳːəllll]

Exercise 6-4

次の文章の中に [l] が 18 個出てきます。下線を引いてみましょう。グレーの語の l は発音されません。

Hello, my name is Ann. I'm taking American Accent Training. There's a lot to learn, but I hope to make it as enjoyable as possible. I should pick up on the American intonation pattern pretty easily, although the only way to get it is to practice all of the time. I use the up and down, or peaks and valleys, intonation more than I used to. I've been paying attention to pitch, too. It's like walking down a staircase. I've been talking to a lot of Americans lately, and they tell me that I'm easier to understand. Anyway, I could go on and on, but the important thing is to listen well and sound good. Well, what do you think? Do I?

Exercise 6-5   CD 2-23

舌先をしっかり歯茎につける練習をしましょう。舌先を歯茎につけ、舌の両側から息を出し続けながら次の文を何度も発音してみましょう（もちろんこれでは [l] 以外の音を正確に発音することはできませんが、そこはあまり気にする必要はありません）。

Leave a little for Lola!

Exercise 6-6   CD 2-24

次の文章を [l] に注意しながら音声の後について発音してみましょう。

Little Lola felt left out in life. She told herself that luck controlled her and she truly believed that only by loyally following an exalted leader could she be delivered from her solitude. Unfortunately, she learned a little late that her life was her own to deal with. When she realized it, she was already eligible for Social Security and she had lent her lifelong earnings to a lowlife in Long Beach. She lay on her linoleum and slid along the floor in anguish. A little later, she leapt up and laughed. She no longer longed for a leader to tell her how to live her life. Little Lola was finally all well.

語末に出てくる [l] の練習です。音声の後について上から下に向かって繰り返し発音してみましょう。

* アメリカ英語では [t] の後に [l] が続くときも Unit 5 で見た「語中の T」のルールが適用されることがあります。

[ʊl]	[ɑːl]	[aʊl]	[el]	[eɪl]	[oʊl]	[iːl]	[dl]
1. bull	ball	bowel	bell	bale	bowl	Beal	bottle
2.	hall	howl	hell	hail	hole	heel	huddle
3.	hauled	howled	held	hailed	hold	healed	hurtle
4. pull	pall	Powell	pell	pail	pole	peel	poodle
5. wool	wall		well	whale	whole	wheel	wheedle
6. full	fall	foul	fell	fail	foal	feel	fetal
7. Schultz	shawl		shell	shale	shoal	she'll	shuttle
8. tulle	tall	towel	tell	tale	toll	teal	turtle
9.	vault	vowel	veldt	veil	vole	veal	vital
10. you'll	yawl	yowl	yell	Yale		yield	yodel
11.	call	cowl	Kelly	kale	cold	keel	coddle

2 | まとめ

次の文章を子音＋ [l] の音連続に注意しながら、音声の後について発音してみましょう。

Thirty Little Turtles in a Bottle of Bottled Water

A bottle of bottled water held 30 little turtles. It didn't matter that each turtle had to rattle a metal ladle in order to get a little bit of noodles, a total turtle delicacy. The problem was that there were many turtle battles for the less than oodles of noodles. The littlest turtles always lost, because every time they thought about grappling with the haggler turtles, their little turtle minds boggled and they only caught a little bit of noodles.

これまで何度も練習してきた文章をできるだけ早いスピードで読んでみましょう。まず、1) 音声のモデルを聞いた後、同じようなスピードで 5 回読んでください。2) 次にモデルが 1 文ずつ読み上げるので、その後に続いて同じスピードで発音してください。3) 最後に自分の声を録音して同じような発音ができたか確認してみましょう。

Hello, **my** name is Ann. I'm taking American **Accent** Training. There's a **lot** to learn, but I **hope** to make it as **enjoyable** as possible. I should pick **up** on the American **intonation** pattern pretty **easily**, although the **only** way to **get** it is to **practice** all of the time. I use the **up** and down, or **peaks** and valleys, **intonation** more than I **used** to. I've been paying attention to **pitch**, **too**. It's like **walking** down a **stair**case. I've been **talking** to a lot of **Americans** lately, and they tell me that I'm **easier** to under**stand**. **Any**way, I could go **on** and on, but the **important** thing is to **listen** well and sound **good**. **Well**, what do you **think**? **Do** I?

次は同じ文章を、音声のモデルと一緒に（＝ほぼ同時に）読んでみましょう。

Hello, **my** name is Ann. I'm taking American **Accent** Training. There's a **lot** to learn, but I **hope** to make it as **enjoyable** as possible. I should pick **up** on the American **intonation** pattern pretty **easily**, although the **only** way to **get** it is to **practice** all of the time. I use the **up** and down, or **peaks** and valleys, **intonation** more than I **used** to. I've been paying attention to **pitch**, **too**. It's like **walking** down a **stair**case. I've been **talking** to a lot of **Americans** lately, and they tell me that I'm **easier** to under**stand**. **Any**way, I could go **on** and on, but the **important** thing is to **listen** well and sound **good**. **Well**, what do you **think**? **Do** I?

UNIT 7

R の発音

1 R の発音

発音方法

舌先を口の天井に向けて少しそり返らせ、声帯を振動させながら息を出し続けます。語頭に出てきたときは、唇を少し丸めてみてください。舌が歯茎に当たらないよう注意しましょう。

Exercise 7-1   CD 2-29

[g] の後に [r] が続く単語などの練習をしましょう。[g] を発音するときは舌の後方部をのどの奥に密着させますが、このときに同時に舌先を巻き上げてください。[g] と [r] の間に母音が入った「グラ」のようにならないように気をつけましょう。音声の後について繰り返し発音してみましょう。

[g], [gr], Greek, green, grass, grow, crow, core, cork, coral, cur, curl, girl, gorilla, her, erg, error, mirror, were, war, gore, wrong, wringer, church, pearl

2 母音 + [ɚ] の発音

アメリカ英語独特の母音、あいまい母音の [ə] に [r] の音色が加わった [ɚ] の練習してみましょう。

Exercise 7-2   CD 2-30

母音 + [ɚ] を含む単語の発音を練習してみましょう。少し大げさな発音になっていますが、音声の後について左から右へと発音してみましょう。

1	2	3
[ɑ] + [ɚ]	[hɑ•ɚd]	hard
[ɪ] + [ɚ]	[hɪ•ɚ]	here
[e] + [ɚ]	[ʃe•ɚ]	share
[ɔ] + [ɚ]	[mɔ•ɚ]	more
[ɚ] + [ɚ]	[wɚ•ɚ]	were

Exercise 7-3　　　　　　　　　　　　　　　　　　　　CD 2-31

次に、Exercise 7-2 のグループ 3 の単語を順番に発音してみましょう。今度は母音＋ [ɚ] をスムーズに発音してみましょう。

hard　here　share　more　were

Exercise 7-4　　　　　　　　　　　　　　　　　　　　CD 2-32

[ɚ] を含む単語で、発音が難しいものをいくつか練習してみましょう。

1. were　　　　　[wɚˑɚ]
   これは [ɚ] を引き伸ばした感じで発音します。[ɚ] が 2 個分あるという気持ちで発音してください。

2. word　　　　　[wɚˑɚd]
   これは、were の後に [d] をつけただけですが、[d] は語末なので破裂しない場合もあります。

3. whirl　　　　　[wɚˑɚəl]
   Unit 6 で見たように語末の [l] の前には [ə] を入れて発音してみてください。

4. world/whirled　　[wɚˑɚəld]
   3. の [wɚˑɚəl] の後に [d] をつけ足します。

5. wore/war　　　[wɔˑɚ]
   [ɔ] と [ɚ] の 2 つの母音が連続する感じです。

6. whorl　　　　　[wɔˑɚəl]
   5. の [wɔˑɚ] の後に [l] が続くので、その前に [ə] をつけ足します。

7. where/wear　　[weˑɚ]
   5. の [wɔˑɚ] とほぼ同じですが、母音が [ɔ] から [e] に変わっています。

音声をよく聞いて 1.〜7. までの単語を繰り返してみましょう。

[ɚʳ(ː)] や母音＋[ɚʳ] を含む単語の発音練習です。音声の後について上から下に向かって繰り返し発音してみましょう。

	[ɚʳ(ː)]	[ɑɚʳ]	[eɚʳ]	[ɔɚʳ]	[ɪɚʳ]	[aʊɚʳ]
1.	earn	art	air	or	ear	hour
2.	hurt	heart	hair	horse	here	how're
3.	heard	hard	haired	horde	here's	
4.	pert	part	pair	pour	peer	power
5.	word		where	war	we're	
6.	a word		aware	award	a weird	
7.	work		wear	warm	weird	
8.	first	far	fair	four	fear	flower
9.	firm	farm	fairy	form	fierce	
10.	rather	cathartic	there	Thor	theory	11th hour
11.	murky	mar	mare	more	mere	
12.	spur	spar	spare	sport	spear	
13.	sure	sharp	share	shore	shear	shower
14.	churn	char	chair	chore	cheer	
15.	gird	guard	scared	gored	geared	Gower
16.	cur	car	care	core	kir	cower
17.	turtle	tar	tear	tore	tear	tower
18.	dirt	dark	dare	door	dear	dour
19.	stir	star	stair	store	steer	
20.	sir	sorry	Sarah	sore	seer	sour
21.	burn	barn	bear	born	beer	bower

3 母音＋[r] の発音

AR という文字列を含む単語の発音練習です。音声の後について上から下に向かって繰り返し発音してみましょう。

embarrass	parallel	parrot
vocabulary	paragraph	apparent
parent	para-	parish

Paris	maritime	Sarah
area	barrier	narrate
aware	baritone	guarantee
compare	Barron's	larynx
imaginary	library	laryngitis
stationary	character	necessary
care	Karen	itinerary
carry	Harry	transparency
carriage	Mary	dictionary
marriage	Larry	

4 まとめ

Exercise 7-7   CD 2-35

[r] に注意しながら次の文章を音声の後について発音してみましょう。

The Mirror Store

The Hurly Burly Mirror Store at Vermont and Beverly featured hundreds of first-rate mirrors. There were several mirrors on the chest of drawers, and the largest one was turned toward the door in order to make the room look bigger. One of the girls who worked there was concerned that a bird might get hurt by hurtling into its own reflection. She learned by trial and error how to preserve both the mirrors and birds. Her earnings were proportionately increased at the mirror store to reflect her contribution to the greater good.

Exercise 7-8

次の文章の中に出てくる [r] に下線を引いてみましょう。例として最初に出てきた [r] にはすでに下線が引いてあります。

Hello, **my** name is Ann. I'm taking American **Accent** Training. There's a **lot** to learn, but I **hope** to make it as **enjoyable** as possible. I should pick **up** on the American **intonation** pattern pretty **easily**, although the **only** way to **get** it is to **practice** all of the time. I use the **up** and down, or **peaks** and valleys, **intonation** more than I **used** to. I've been paying attention to **pitch, too**. It's like **walking** down a **stair**case. I've been **talking** to a lot of **Americans** lately, and they tell me that I'm **easier** to under**stand**. **Any**way, I could go **on** and on, but the **important** thing is to **listen** well and sound **good**. **Well**, what do you **think**? **Do** I?

UNIT 8

長い語句のアクセント

Unit 2 の内容を復習した後、少し長い語句のアクセントパターンを練習しましょう。

1　2 語からなる語句のアクセントパターン

Exercise 8-1　　　　　　　　　　　　　　　　　　　　　　　　CD 2-36

形容詞と名詞からなる普通の名詞句では、2 つ目の語がアクセントを受け、複合名詞になる場合は、最初の語がアクセントを受けました。Unit 2 の Exercise 2-11 を使って復習してみましょう。音声の後について発音してみましょう。

名詞句	複合名詞
1. It's a short **nail**.	It's a **finger**nail.
2. It's a chocolate **cake**.	It's a **pan**cake.
3. It's a hot **bath**.	It's a **hot** tub.
4. It's a long **drive**.	It's a **hard** drive.
5. It's the back **door**.	It's the **back**bone.
6. There are four **cards**.	It's a **card** trick.
7. It's a small **spot**.	It's a **spot**light.
8. It's a good **book**.	It's a **phone** book.

Exercise 8-2　　　　　　　　　　　　　　　　　　　　　　　　CD 2-37

下線部の語句のアクセントを受ける単語を○で囲んでみましょう。その後、音声の後について発音してみましょう。

1. They live in <u>Los Angeles</u>.
2. Give me a <u>paper bag</u>.
3. Is that your <u>lunch bag</u>?
4. 7-11 is a <u>convenience store</u>.
5. Lucky's is a <u>convenient store</u>.
6. Do your <u>homework</u>!
7. He's a <u>good writer</u>.
8. It's an <u>apple pie</u>.
9. It's a <u>pineapple</u>.
10. We like <u>all things</u>.
11. We like <u>everything</u>.
12. It's a <u>moving van</u>.

13. It's a <u>new paper</u>.

14. It's the <u>newspaper</u>.

15. The doll has <u>glass eyes</u>.

16. The doll has <u>eyeglasses</u>.

17. It's a <u>high chair</u>.

18. It's a <u>highchair</u>. *(for babies)*

19. It's a <u>baseball</u>.

20. It's a <u>blue ball</u>.

2 ｜ 3 語からなる語句のアクセントパターン

Exercise 8-3 CD 2-38

普通の名詞句を形容詞や副詞で修飾するときは、名詞句のアクセントパターンはそのままにして、<u>形容詞や副詞にもアクセントを置きます</u>。音声の後について発音してみましょう。

名詞句	修飾語＋名詞句
1. It's a short **nail**.	It's a **really** short **nail**.
2. It's a chocolate **cake**.	It's a **tasty** chocolate **cake**.
3. I took a hot **bath**.	I took a **long**, hot **bath**.
4. It's a hard **drive**.	It's a **long**, hard **drive**.
5. It's the back **door**.	It's the **only** back **door**.
6. There are four **cards**.	There are **four** slick **cards**.
7. It's a little **spot**.	It's a **little** black **spot**.
8. It's a good **book**.	It's a **really** good **book**.

Exercise 8-4 CD 2-39

複合名詞を形容詞で修飾するときは、複合名詞のアクセントパターンはそのままですが、<u>形容詞にはアクセントを置きません</u>。音声の後について発音してみましょう。

複合名詞	形容詞＋複合名詞
1. It's a **finger**nail.	It's a short **finger**nail.
2. It's a **pan**cake.	It's a delicious **pan**cake.
3. It's a **hot** tub.	It's a leaky **hot** tub.
4. It's a **hard** drive.	It's an expensive **hard** drive.
5. It's the **back**bone.	It's a long **back**bone.
6. It's a **card** trick.	It's a clever **card** trick.
7. It's a **spot**light.	It's a bright **spot**light.
8. It's a **phone** book.	It's the new **phone** book.

Exercise 8-5   CD 2-40

複合名詞は2語でも3語でも、最初の語がアクセントを受けることに変わりありません。音声の後について発音してみましょう。

2語からなる複合名詞	3語からなる複合名詞
1. It's a **finger**nail.	It's a **finger**nail clipper.
2. It's a **pan**cake.	It's a **pan**cake shop.
3. It's a **hot** tub.	It's a **hot** tub maker.
4. It's a **hard** drive.	It's a **hard** drive holder.
5. It's the **back**bone.	It's a **back**bone massage.
6. It's a **playing** card.	It's a **playing** card rack.
7. It's a **spot**light.	It's a **spot**light stand.
8. It's a **phone** book.	It's a **phone** book listing.

Exercise 8-6   CD 2-41

3語からなる語句のおさらいです。音声の後について発音してみましょう。

修飾語＋名詞句	形容詞＋複合名詞	3語からなる複合名詞
1. a **really** short **nail**	a long **finger**nail	a **finger**nail clipper
2. a **big** chocolate **cake**	a thin **pan**cake	a **pan**cake shop
3. a **long**, hot **bath**	a leaky **hot** tub	a **hot** tub maker
4. a **long**, boring **drive**	a new **hard** drive	a **hard** drive holder
5. a **broken** back **door**	a long **back**bone	a **back**bone massage
6. **four** slick **cards**	a new **playing** card	a **playing** card rack
7. a **small** black **spot**	a bright **spot**light	a **spot**light stand
8. a **well**-written **book**	an open **phone** book	a **phone** book listing
9.	a blind **sales**man	a **blind** salesman
	(He can't see.)	*(He sells blinds.)*
10.	a light **house**keeper	a **light**house keeper
	(She cleans the house.)	*(She lives in a lighthouse.)*
11.	a green **house**plant	a **green**house plant
	(It's a healthy houseplant.)	*(It's from a greenhouse.)*

3 語からなる語句を含む短い物語を読んでみましょう。音声の後について発音してみましょう。

Once upon a time, there were *three little pigs*. They lived with their *kind old mother* near a *large*, *dark forest*. One day, they decided to build *their own houses*. The *first little pig* used straw. He took his *straw-cutting tools* and his *new lawnmower*, and built a *little straw house*. The *second little pig* used sticks. He took his *woodcutting tools* and some *old paintbrushes,* and built a *small wooden house*. The *third little pig*, who was a *very hard worker*, used bricks. He took his *bricklaying tools*, an *expensive mortarboard*, and built a *large brick house*. In the forest, lived a *big bad wolf*. He wanted to eat the *three little pigs*, so he went to the *flimsy straw abode* and tried to blow it down. "Not by the hair of my *chinny chin chin*!" cried the *three little porkers*. But the house was *not very strong*, and the *big bad beast* blew it down. The *three little pigs* ran to the *rickety wooden structure*, but the *big bad wolf* blew it down, too. Quickly, the *three little piggies* ran to the *sturdy brick dwelling* and hid inside. The *big bad wolf* huffed and he puffed, but he couldn't blow the *strong brick house* down. The *three little pigs* laughed and danced and sang.

普通の名詞句や動詞句（動詞＋副詞）は 2 つ目の語がアクセントを受けるのが原則ですが、文の強弱リズムを維持しやすくするため、アクセントが 1 つ目の語に移動することがあります。下線の引いてある語句は本来 2 つ目の語にアクセントが来ますが、1 つ目の語に移動しています（アクセントが移動することで意味は変わりません）。音声の後について発音してみましょう。

There is a *little girl* called *Goldilocks*. She is *walking through* a *sunny forest* and sees a *small house*. She *knocks* on the door, but *no one* answers. She *goes inside* to see what's there. There are *three chairs* in the *large room*. *Goldilocks* sits on the *biggest chair*. It's *too high* for her to *sit on*. She sits on the *middle-sized* one, but it's *too low*. She sits on the *small chair* and it is *just right*. On the table, there are *three bowls* of porridge. She tries the *first one*, but it's *too hot* to swallow. The *second one* is *too cold*, and the *third one* is *just right*, so she eats it all. *After that*, she *goes upstairs* to *look around*. There are *three beds* in the *bedroom*. She *sits down* on the *biggest one*. It's *too hard* to *sleep on*. The *middle-sized* bed is *too soft*. The *little one* is *just right*, so she *lies down* and *falls asleep*.

In the *meantime*, the family of *three bears* come home—the *Papa bear*, the *Mama bear*, and the *Baby bear*. They *look around* and say, "Who's been sitting on our chairs and eating our porridge?" Then they *run upstairs* and say, "Who's been sleeping in our beds?" *Goldilocks* *wakes up* when she hears all the noise and is *so scared* that she *runs out* of the house and never *comes back*.

3　4 語からなる語句のアクセントパターン

Exercise 8-9　　　　　　　　　　　　　　　　　　　　　　　　　　　　CD 2-44

「修飾語＋ 2 語からなる複合名詞」にさらに修飾語を加えるときは、<u>その修飾語にアクセントを</u>
<u>置きます</u>。音声の後について発音してみましょう。

＊ brand new は本来 new にアクセントを置く複合形容詞ですが、名詞を修飾する場合は brand にアクセントが
　置かれます。

修飾語＋複合名詞	修飾語＋修飾語＋複合名詞
1. It's a short **finger**nail.	It's a **really** short **finger**nail.
2. It's a banana **pan**cake.	It's a **tasty** banana **pan**cake.
3. It's a leaky **hot** tub.	It's a **leaky** old **hot** tub.
4. It's a new **hard** drive.	It's a **brand** new **hard** drive.
5. It's a long **back**bone.	It's a **long**, hard **back**bone.
6. It's a wrinkled **playing** card.	It's a **wrinkled**, old **playing** card.
7. It's a bright **spot**light.	It's a **bright** white **spot**light.
8. It's the new **phone** book.	It's a **new** age **phone** book.

Exercise 8-10　　　　　　　　　　　　　　　　　　　　　　　　　　　CD 2-45

3 語からなる複合語にさらに修飾語を加えても、<u>修飾語はアクセントを受けません</u>。音声の後
について発音してみましょう。

3 語からなる複合語	修飾語＋ 3 語からなる複合語
1. It's a **finger**nail clipper.	It's a new **finger**nail clipper.
2. It's a **pan**cake shop.	It's a good **pan**cake shop.
3. He's a **hot** tub maker.	He's the best **hot** tub maker.
4. It's a **hard** drive holder.	It's a plastic **hard** drive holder.
5. It's a **back**bone massage.	It's a painful **back**bone massage.
6. It's a **playing** card rack.	It's my best **playing** card rack.
7. It's a **spot**light bulb.	It's a fragile **spot**light bulb.
8. It's a **phone** book listing.	It's an unusual **phone** book listing.

4 語からなる語句を含む短い物語を読んでみましょう。音声の後について発音してみましょう。

Once upon a time, there was a *cute little redhead* named *Little Red Riding Hood*. One day, she told her mother that she wanted to take a *well-stocked picnic basket* to her *dear old grandmother* on the other side of the *dark, scary Black Forest*. Her mother warned her not to talk to strangers—especially the *dangerous big bad wolf*. *Little Red Riding Hood* said she would be careful, and left. Halfway there, she saw a *mild-mannered hitchhiker*. She pulled over in her *bright red sports car* and offered him a ride. Just before they got to the *freeway turnoff* for her *old grandmother's house*, the *heavily bearded young man* jumped out and ran away. (Was he the wolf?) He hurried ahead to the *waiting grandmother's house*, let himself in, ate her, and jumped into her bed to wait for *Little Red Riding Hood*. When *Little Red Riding Hood* got to the house, she was surprised, "Grandmother, what big *eyes* you have!" The wolf replied, "The better to *see* you with, my dear . . ." "But Grandmother, what big *ears* you have!" "The better to *hear* you with, my dear . . ." "Oh, Grandmother, what big *teeth* you have!" "The better to *eat* you with!" And the wolf jumped out of the bed to eat *Little Red Riding Hood*. Fortunately for her, she was a *recently paid-up member* of the *infamous National Rifle Association* so she pulled out her *brand new shotgun* and shot the wolf dead.

4 | まとめ

1. ～ 11. の文をアクセントに注意しながら、音声の後について発音してみましょう。また、自分でも同じようなパターンの文を作ってみてください。

1. It's a **pot**.   （名詞）
2. It's **new**.   （形容詞）
3. It's a new **pot**.   （形容詞＋名詞）
4. brand **new**   （修飾語＋形容詞）
5. It's a **brand** new **pot**.   （修飾語＋修飾語＋名詞）
6. It's a **tea**pot.   （2 語からなる複合名詞）
7. It's a new **tea**pot.   （形容詞＋複合名詞）
8. It's a **brand** new **tea**pot.   （修飾語＋修飾語＋複合名詞）

9. It's a **tea**pot lid.   (3 語からなる複合名詞)
10. It's a new **tea**pot lid.   (形容詞＋3 語からなる複合名詞)
11. It's a **brand** new **tea**pot lid. (修飾語＋修飾語＋3 語からなる複合名詞)

1. _____ (名詞)
2. _____ (形容詞)
3. _____ (形容詞＋名詞)
4. _____ (修飾語＋形容詞)
5. _____ (修飾語＋修飾語＋名詞)
6. _____ (2 語からなる複合名詞)
7. _____ (形容詞＋複合名詞)
8. _____ (修飾語＋修飾語＋複合名詞)
9. _____ (3 語からなる複合名詞)
10. _____ (形容詞＋3 語からなる複合名詞)
11. _____ (修飾語＋修飾語＋3 語からなる複合名詞)

UNIT 9

応用練習

これまでに習ったことを復習しながら、次の文章をネイティブらしく発音する練習を
してみましょう。

Ignorance on Parade

You say you don't know a proton from a crouton? Well, you're not the only one. A
recent nationwide survey funded by the National Science Foundation shows that fewer
than 6 percent of American adults can be called scientifically literate. The rest think
that DNA is a food additive, Chernobyl is a ski resort, and radioactive milk can be
made safe by boiling. (from Judith Stone / 1989 Discover Publications)

Exercise 9-1

まず、Unit 2 の 3. や Unit 8 で習った、名詞句、複合名詞、対比の違いなどに注意しながら、
アクセントを受ける単語に下線を引いてみましょう。

Ignorance on Parade

You say you don't know a proton from a crouton? Well, you're not the only one. A
recent nationwide survey funded by the National Science Foundation shows that fewer
than 6 percent of American adults can be called scientifically literate. The rest think
that DNA is a food additive, Chernobyl is a ski resort, and radioactive milk can be
made safe by boiling.

Exercise 9-2

次に Unit 2 の 6. で習ったアイデアグループに区切ってみます。ポーズを入れた方がよい思う
ところに斜線を入れてみましょう。

Ignorance on Parade

You say you don't know a proton from a crouton? Well, you're not the only one. A
recent nationwide survey funded by the National Science Foundation shows that fewer
than 6 percent of American adults can be called scientifically literate. The rest think
that DNA is a food additive, Chernobyl is a ski resort, and radioactive milk can be
made safe by boiling.

Exercise 9-3

次に Unit 3 で習った音の連結、脱落、スムーズ化、同化が起こる個所を探してみましょう。

Ignorance on Parade

You say you don't know a proton from a crouton? Well, you're not the only one. A recent nationwide survey funded by the National Science Foundation shows that fewer than 6 percent of American adults can be called scientifically literate. The rest think that DNA is a food additive, Chernobyl is a ski resort, and radioactive milk can be made safe by boiling.

Exercise 9-4

ハイライトペンを使い、Unit 4 で習った 3 つの母音のうち、[æ] には青色、[ɑ] には緑色、[ə] には赤色の線を引いてみましょう。

Ignorance on Parade

You say you don't know a proton from a crouton? Well, you're not the only one. A recent nationwide survey funded by the National Science Foundation shows that fewer than 6 percent of American adults can be called scientifically literate. The rest think that DNA is a food additive, Chernobyl is a ski resort, and radioactive milk can be made safe by boiling.

Exercise 9-5

T にはいろいろな発音があることを Unit 5 で習いました。文中に出てくる T はどのように発音されるか、書き入れてみましょう。

Ignorance on Parade

You say you don't know a proton from a crouton? Well, you're not the only one. A recent nationwide survey funded by the National Science Foundation shows that fewer than 6 percent of American adults can be called scientifically literate. The rest think that DNA is a food additive, Chernobyl is a ski resort, and radioactive milk can be made safe by boiling.

UNIT 10

V, TH, S/Z の発音

ここでは、口の前方で発音する子音を練習します。

1 | V の発音

発音方法
上の歯を下唇の内側に軽く当て、声帯を振動させながら、息を吐き出します。

唇を使って出す音は、[v] 以外にも [w], [b], [p], [f] の 4 つの音があります。[w] は Unit 3 で唇を突き出して発音する「わたり音」として出てきました。日本人は [v] を [b] と混同しがちなので注意が必要です。[b] は発音するときの口の構え（＝発音位置）も息の出し方も [v] とは異なります。また、[f] を日本語の [ɸ]（＝「フ」の子音部）で発音しないよう注意してください。それぞれの音は次のような関係にあります。

発音位置		両唇		唇歯	
声帯の振動		有声	無声	有声	無声
息の出し方	破裂	[b]	[p]		
	摩擦		[ɸ]	[v]	[f]

Exercise 10-1 box and CD 2-48

Exercise 10-1 CD 2-48

音声の後について繰り返し発音してみましょう。リストは、まず上から下に向かって、その後、左から右に向かって読まれています。

P	B	F	V	W
1. Perry	berry	fairy	very	wary
2. pat	bat	fat	vat	wax
3. Paul	ball	fall	vault	wall
4. pig	big	fig	vim	wig
5. prayed	braid	frayed		weighed

P	B	F	V	W
6. poi	boy	foil	avoid	▓▓▓
7. pull	bull	full	▓▓▓	wool
8. purr	burr	fur	verb	were

[v] と [w] に注意しながら次の文章を音声の後について発音してみましょう。

When re**v**ising his **v**isitor's **v**ersion o**f** a plan for a **v**ery **w**ell-pa**v**ed a**v**enue, the **V**IP **w**as ad**v**ised to re**v**eal none o**f** his moti**v**es. **E**ventually, howe**v**er, the hapless **v**isitor disco**v**ered his kna**v**ish **v**iews and confined that it **w**as **v**ital to re**v**iew the plans together to a**v**oid a conflict. The **V**IP **w**as not con**v**inced, and a**v**erred that he **w**ould ha**v**e it **v**etoed by the **v**ice president. This quite **v**exed the **v**isitor, who then **v**owed to in**v**ent an indestructible pa**v**ing compound in order to a**v**enge his good name. The **V**IP found himself on the **v**erge o**f** a ci**v**il **w**ar **w**ith a **v**isitor **w**ith whom he had pre**v**iously con**v**ersed easily. It **w**as only due to his insufferable **v**anity that the ine**v**itable di**v**ision arri**v**ed as soon as it did. Ne**v**er again did the **v**isitor con**v**erse **w**ith the **v**ain **V**IP and they remained di**v**ided fore**v**er.

次の文章の中に [v] の音は5つあります。下線を引いてみましょう。最初に出てきた [v] にはすでに下線が引いてあります。

Hello, **my** name is Ann. I'm taking American **Accent** Training. There's a **lot** to learn, but I **hope** to make it as **enjoyable** as possible. I should pick **up** on the American **intonation** pattern pretty **easily**, although the **only** way to **get** it is to **practice** all o**f** the time. I use the **up** and down, or **peaks** and valleys, **intonation** more than I **used** to. I've been paying attention to **pitch**, **too**. It's like **walking** down a **stair**case. I've been **talking** to a lot of **Americans** lately, and they tell me that I'm **easier** to under**stand**. **Any**way, I could go **on** and on, but the **important** thing is to **listen** well and sound **good**. **Well**, what do you **think**? **Do** I?

2 | TH の発音

発音方法

舌先を上下の歯の間から軽く突き出した後、すぐに戻します。声帯を振動させながら発音すると有声音の [ð]、振動させずに発音すると無声音の [θ] になります。

日本人が苦手とする発音の1つですが、舌先を上の歯の裏に近づけて（または軽く触れて）、そこから息を出しても同じ音として通じます。

Exercise 10-4　　　　　　　　　　　　　　　　　　　　　　　　　　　CD 2-50

音声をよく聞き、その後、繰り返して発音してみましょう。[ð] と発音されるのは 17 個、[θ] と発音されるのは 44 個あります。[ð] と発音される所は太字になっています。

The throng of thermometers from **the** Thuringian Thermometer Folks arrived on Thursday. **Th**ere were a thousand thirty-three thick thermometers, **th**ough, instead of a thousand thirty-six thin thermometers, which was three thermometers fewer **than the** thousand thirty-six we were expecting, not to mention **th**at **t**hey were thick ones ra**th**er **th**an thin ones. We thoroughly thought **th**at we had ordered a thousand thirty-six, not a thousand thirty-three, thermometers, and asked **the** Thuringian Thermometer Folks to reship **th**e thermometers; thin, not thick. **Th**ey apologized for sending only a thousand thirty-three thermometers ra**th**er **th**an a thousand thirty-six and promised to replace **the** thick thermometers with thin thermometers.

Exercise 10-5

TH の音を意識する練習です。まず、次の文章を、実際に口は動かしますが、声は出さずに読んでみましょう。そのときに、手鏡などを使って TH を発音するときの口の様子を確認してみてください。その後、文章内に出てくる TH の音に下線を引いてみましょう。有声の [ð] は 10 個、無声の [θ] は 2 個あります。

Hello, **my** name is Ann. I'm taking American **Accent** Training. There's a **lot** to learn, but I **hope** to make it as **enjoyable** as possible. I should pick **up** on the American **intonation** pattern pretty **easily**, although the **only** way to **get** it is to **practice** all of the time. I use the **up** and down, or **peaks** and valleys, **intonation** more than I **used** to. I've been paying attention to **pitch**, **too**. It's like **walking** down a **stair**case. I've been **talking** to a lot of **Americans** lately, and they tell me that I'm **easier** to under**stand**. **Any**way, I could go **on** and on, but the **important** thing is to **listen** well and sound **good**. **Well**, what do you **think**? **Do** I?

V, TH, S/Z の発音　93

最後に TH を含む早口ことばにチャレンジしてみましょう！

1. The sixth sick Sheik's sixth thick sheep.
2. This is a zither. Is this a zither?
3. I thought a **thought**. But the thought I **thought** wasn't the thought I **thought** I thought. If the thought I **thought** I thought had been the thought I **thought**, I wouldn't have **thought** so much.

3　S/Z の発音

発音方法
舌先を歯茎に近づけ、息を吐き出します。声帯を振動させなければ無声音の [s]、振動させれば有声音の [z] になります。

音声の後について繰り返し発音してみましょう。 Unit 4 で見たように、母音の長さは、有声子音よりも無声子音が続くときの方が短くなることにも注意しましょう。

S	Z
1. price	prize
2. peace	peas
3. place	plays
4. ice	eyes
5. hiss	his
6. close	to close
7. use	to use
8. rice	rise
9. pace	pays
10. lacey	lazy
11. thirsty	Thursday
12. bus	buzz
13. dust	does
14. face	phase
15. Sue	zoo
16. loose	lose

[s] を含む次の文章を、音声の後について繰り返し発音してみましょう。

Sam, a surly sergeant from Cisco, Texas, saw a sailor sit silently on a small seat reserved for youngsters. He stayed for several minutes, while tots swarmed around. Sam asked the sailor to cease and desist but he sneered in his face. Sam was so incensed that he considered it sufficient incentive to sock the sailor. The sailor stood there for a second, astonished, and then strolled away. Sam was perplexed, but satisfied, and the tots scampered like ants over to the seesaw.

[z] を含む次の文章を、音声の後について繰り返し発音してみましょう。

A lazy Thursday at the zoo found the zebras grazing on zinnias, posing for pictures, and teasing the zookeeper, whose nose was bronzed by the sun. The biggest zebra's name was Zachary, but his friends called him Zack. Zack was a confusing zebra whose zeal for reason caused his cousins, who were naturally unreasoning, to pause in their conversations. While they browsed, he philosophized. As they grazed, he practiced Zen. Because they were Zack's cousins, the zebras said nothing, but they wished he would muzzle himself at times.

used の発音

use は -ed が続くとき、[ju:st] と [ju:zd] の 2 通りの発音があります。

[ju:st] になるとき
- 過去の習慣　　　　　　　　I used to eat rice.
- 「慣れている」という意味　I am used to eating rice.

[ju:zd] になるとき
- 過去形　　　　　　　　　　I used chopsticks to eat rice.
- 受け身形　　　　　　　　　Chopsticks are used to eat rice.

次の文章の中に出てくる [s] の音に下線を引いてみましょう。次に [z] の音に○をつけてみましょう。スペリングに惑わされないよう注意しましょう。

Hello, **my** name is Ann. I'm taking American **Accent** Training. There's a **lot** to learn, but I **hope** to make it as **enjoyable** as possible. I should pick **up** on the American **intonation** pattern pretty **easily**, although the **only** way to **get** it is to **practice** all of the time. I use the **up** and down, or **peaks** and valleys, **intonation** more than I **used** to. I've been paying attention to **pitch, too**. It's like **walking** down a **stair**case. I've been **talking** to a lot of **Americans** lately, and they tell me that I'm **easier** to under**stand**. **Any**way, I could go **on** and on, but the **important** thing is to **listen** well and sound **good**. **Well**, what do you **think**? **Do** I?

UNIT 11

M, N, NG の発音

鼻から息を出して発音する鼻音の練習です。鼻音はすべて有声音です。

発音方法

[m]

[b] を発音するときのように両唇をしっかり閉じたまま、鼻から息を出します。

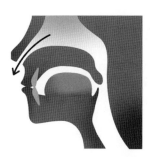

[n]

[d] を発音するときのように舌先を歯茎につけたまま、鼻から息を出します。

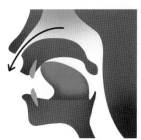

[ŋ]

[g] を発音するときのように舌の後方をのどの奥につけたまま、鼻から息を出します。

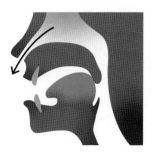

Exercise 11-1   CD 2-55

音声の後について繰り返し発音してみましょう。

＊ 英語では [ŋ] で始まる単語はないため、以下の練習では語句も使っています。

	語頭		語中		語末	
[m]/[b]	me	bee	llama	lobber	ROM	rob
[n]/[d]	knees	deals	Lana	lauder	Ron	rod
[ŋ]/[g]	long eels	geese	longer	logger	wrong	log

Exercise 11-2   CD 2-56

音声の後について繰り返し発音してみましょう。

The you**ng** Ki**ng** Ko**ng** ca**n** si**ng** alo**ng** o**n** anythi**ng** i**n** the ki**ng**dom, as lo**ng** as he ca**n** bri**ng** a stro**ng** ri**ng**ing to the cha**ng**ing so**ng**s. He can o**n**ly trai**n** o**n** June mor**n**i**ng**s whe**n** there is a full moo**n**, but Ju**n**e le**n**ds itself to si**ng**ing like **n**othi**ng** else. Di**ng** Do**ng**, o**n** the other ha**nd**, is **n**ot a si**ng**er; he ca**nn**ot si**ng** for anythi**ng**. He is the ma**n** ofte**n** see**n** o**n** the gree**n** law**n** o**n** the Bosto**n** Ope**n**, where **n**o o**n**e ever, ever si**ng**s.

Exercise 11-3

[n] と [ŋ] と発音される個所に下線を引いてください。

Hello, my name is Ann. I'm taking American **Accent** Training. There's a **lot** to learn, but I **hope** to make it as **enjoyable** as possible. I should pick **up** on the American **intonation** pattern pretty **easily**, although the **only** way to **get** it is to **practice** all of the time. I use the **up** and down, or **peaks** and valleys, **intonation** more than I **used** to. I've been paying attention to **pitch, too**. It's like **walking** down a **stair**case. I've been **talking** to a lot of **Americans** lately, and they tell me that I'm **easier** to under**stand**. **Any**way, I could go **on** and on, but the **important** thing is to **listen** well and sound **good. Well**, what do you **think? Do** I?

UNIT 12

H, K, G, NG の発音

ここではのどの奥の方で発音する子音を練習しましょう。

発音方法

[h]：[h] 自体の口の構えはありません。次に来る音を発音するときの口の構えをしたまま息を出します。声帯は振動させません。

[k]：舌の後方をのどの奥につけて息の流れを完全に止めた後、一気に息を吐き出します。声帯は振動させません。

[g]：[k] と同じ口の構えのまま、声帯を振動させます。

[ŋ]：[g] と同じ口の構えのまま、鼻から息を出します（Unit 11 でも出てきました）。

Exercise 12-1   CD 2-57

音声の後について繰り返し発音してみましょう。

	語頭	語中	語末
[h]	haw	reheat	
	hood	in half	
	he'll	unhinge	
	hat	unheard of	
[k]	caw	accident	rink
	could	accent	rack
	keel	include	cork
	cat	actor	block
[g]	gaw	regale	rug
	good	ingrate	hog
	geese	agree	big
	gat	organ	log

語頭	語中	語末
[ŋ] Long Island	Bronx	wrong
a long wait	inky	daring
Dang you!	larynx	averaging
being honest	English	clung

Exercise 12-2   CD 2-58

X はこの後に続く文字や、アクセントがどこに来るかによって [ks] という発音になったり [gz] という発音になったりします。

[ks] になるとき

X の前の母音にアクセントがある場合

extra	[**eks**trə]
exercise	[**eks**əʳsaɪz]
execute	[**eks**əkjuːt]
excellent	[**eks**ələnt]

[gz] になるとき

X の後の母音にアクセントがある場合

example	[ɪg**zæm**pl]
exist	[ɪg**zɪst**]
exam	[ɪg**zæm**]
exert	[ɪg**zəʳːt**]
examine	[ɪg**zæm**ən]
executive	[ɪg**zek**jətɪv]
exactly	[ɪg**zæk**tli]

ただし、X の後の母音にアクセントがある場合でも、X の後に文字の C または無声子音が続くときは [ks] になる。

excite	[ek**saɪt**]
experience	[eks**pɪə**ʳiəns]
except	[ek**sept**]

Exercise 12-3   CD 2-59

音声の後について繰り返し発音してみましょう。

H

"Help!" hissed the harried intern. "We have to hurry! The halfwit who was hired to help her home hit her hard with the Honda. She didn't have a helmet on her head to protect her, so she has to have a checkup ahead of the others."

K

The computer cursor careened across the screen, erasing key characters as it scrolled past. The technician was equally confused by the computer technology and the complicated keyboard, so he clicked off the computer, cleaned off his desk, accepted his paycheck, and caught a taxicab for the airport, destination Caracas.

G

The Wizard of Og

There was a man named . . .	Og
Who was his best friend?	Dog
Where did he live?	Bog
What was his house made of?	Log
Who was his neighbor?	Frog
What did he drink?	Eggnog
What did he do for fun?	Jog
What is the weather in his swamp?	Fog

NG

The stunning woman would not have a fling with a strong young flamingo trainer until she had a ring on her finger. He was angry because he longed for her. She inquired if he were hungry, but he hung his head in a funk. The flamingo trainer banged his fist on the fish tank and sang out, "Dang it, I'm sunk without you, Punkin!" She took in a long, slow lungful of air and sighed.

Exercise 12-4

[h], [k], [g], [ŋ] と発音される個所に下線を引いてみましょう。

Hello, my name is Ann. I'm taking American **Accent** Training. There's a **lot** to learn, but I **hope** to make it as **enjoyable** as possible. I should pick **up** on the American **intonation** pattern pretty **easily**, although the **only** way to **get** it is to **practice** all of the time. I use the **up** and down, or **peaks** and valleys, **intonation** more than I **used** to. I've been paying attention to **pitch, too**. It's like **walking** down a **stair**case. I've been **talking** to a lot of **Americans** lately, and they tell me that I'm **easier** to understand. **Anyway**, I could go **on** and on, but the **important** thing is to **listen** well and sound **good**. **Well**, what do you **think**? **Do** I?

UNIT 13

長い文をリズミカルに読む

Unit 1、Unit 2、Unit 8で習ったことを思い出しながら、これまでよりも長い文を英語らしく発音する練習をしてみましょう。

Exercise 13-1   CD 2-60

動詞句がどれほど複雑になっても、Unit 1で習った **Dogs** eat **bones**. の基本アクセントを忘れないでください。名詞句の場合は、普通名詞句のアクセントパターン（convenient **store**）と複合名詞のアクセントパターン（**convenience** store）をきちんと区別することが大切です。まず、The millionaires were impressed by the equipment. という基本文に、単語をつけ足しながら主語と目的語をどんどん長くしていきます。音声の後について繰り返し発音しましょう。

> **主語**

The **millionaires** . . .

The elderly **millionaires** . . .

The **elderly** Texas **millionaires** . . .

The two **elderly** Texas **millionaires** . . .

> **目的語**

. . . the **equipment**.

. . . **eaves**dropping equipment.

. . . electronic **eaves**dropping equipment.

. . . **sophisticated** electronic **eaves**dropping equipment.

Exercise 13-2   CD 2-61

今度は、動詞部分を膨らませていきます。音声の後について繰り返し練習しましょう。

1. The two **elderly** Texas **millionaires**'re impressed by the **sophisticated** electronic **eaves**dropping equipment.

2. The two **elderly** Texas **millionaires** were impressed by the **sophisticated** electronic **eaves**dropping equipment.

3. At the moment, the two **elderly** Texas **millionaires**'re being impressed by the **sophisticated** electronic **eaves**dropping equipment.

4. The two **elderly** Texas **millionaires**'ll be impressed by the **sophisticated** electronic **eaves**dropping equipment.

5. The two **elderly** Texas **millionaires**'d be impressed by the **sophisticated** electronic **eaves**dropping equipment if there were more practical applications for it.

6. The two **elderly** Texas **millionaires**'d've been impressed by the **sophisticated** electronic **eaves**dropping equipment if there had been more practical applications for it.

7. The two **elderly** Texas **millionaires** that've been so impressed by the **sophisticated** electronic **eaves**dropping equipment are now researching a new program.

8. The two **elderly** Texas **millionaires**'ve been impressed by the **sophisticated** electronic **eaves**dropping equipment for a long time now.

9. The two **elderly** Texas **millionaires**'d been impressed by the **sophisticated** electronic **eaves**dropping equipment long before the burglary was thwarted.

10. The two **elderly** Texas **millionaires**'ll've been thoroughly impressed by the **sophisticated** electronic **eaves**dropping equipment by the time I've done my presentation.

11. The two **elderly** Texas **millionaires** ought to be impressed by the **sophisticated** electronic **eaves**dropping equipment.

12. The two **elderly** Texas **millionaires** should be impressed by the **sophisticated** electronic **eaves**dropping equipment.

13. The two **elderly** Texas **millionaires** shouldn't be too impressed by the **sophisticated** electronic **eaves**dropping equipment.

14. The two **elderly** Texas **millionaires** should've been impressed by the **sophisticated** electronic **eaves**dropping equipment.

15. Given the circumstances, the two **elderly** Texas **millionaires** shouldn't've been that impressed by the **sophisticated** electronic **eaves**dropping equipment.

16. We think that the two **elderly** Texas **millionaires** could easily be impressed by the **sophisticated** electronic **eaves**dropping equipment.

17. No matter what we did, the two **elderly** Texas **millionaires** couldn't be impressed by even the most **sophisticated** electronic **eaves**dropping equipment.

18. The two **elderly** Texas **millionaires** could've been impressed by the **sophisticated** electronic **eaves**dropping equipment, but we're not sure.

19. The two **elderly** Texas **millionaires** couldn't've been impressed by the **sophisticated** electronic **eaves**dropping equipment because they left after five minutes.

20. The two **elderly** Texas **millionaires** might be impressed by the **sophisticated** electronic **eaves**dropping equipment this time around.

21. The two **elderly** Texas **millionaires** might've been impressed by the **sophisticated** electronic **eaves**dropping equipment, but they gave no indication one way or the other.

22. The two **elderly** Texas **millionaires** must be impressed by the **sophisticated** electronic **eaves**dropping equipment because they are considering a huge order.

23. The two **elderly** Texas **millionaires** must have been impressed by the **sophisticated** electronic **eaves**dropping equipment because they ordered so much of it.

24. The two **elderly** Texas **millionaires** can be impressed by the **sophisticated** electronic **eaves**dropping equipment because they don't know much about surveillance.

25. The two **elderly** Texas **millionaires** can't be impressed by the **sophisticated** electronic **eaves**dropping equipment because they invented most of the state-of-the-art technology currently available.

Exercise 13-3	CD 2-62

音声の後について繰り返し発音してみましょう。

Forty years after the end of World War II, Japan and the U.S. are again engaged in conflict. Trade frictions, which began as minor irritants in an otherwise smooth relationship in the 1960s, have gradually escalated over the years.

The conflict is more dangerous than it appears because its real nature is partially hidden. It masquerades as a banal and sometimes grubby dispute over widgets with the stakes being whether American or Japanese big business makes more money.

In truth, the issue is strategic and geopolitical in nature. Japan is once again challenging the U.S., only this time the issue is not China or the Pacific, but world industrial and technological leadership and the military and economic powers which have always been its corollaries. (*By permission of *U.S. News and World Report*)

Exercise 13-4	CD 2-63

次は 2000 年の米大統領選挙共和党候補者による討論会の一部です。本人になったつもりで音声の後について繰り返し発音してみましょう。

<Moderator>
The president tomorrow night is expected in his State of the Union message to propose federal subsidies to help low-income families overcome the so-called digital divide. Is

it an appropriate use of government funds to hand out computers and provide Internet access to those who can't afford it, and if not, why not? We'll begin with Mr. Keyes.

<Mr. Keyes>
"I think this is another case where politicians try to jump on the bandwagon of something that's going on in the economy, so everybody's going to think that they actually have something to do with the result when they don't. There's no need for this. We're already seeing out there proposals for the distribution of free PCs, not based on some politician making a judgment and spending taxpayer money, but based on the self-interest of those who are involved in a new world, a new world in which participation is the key to profit—and in which there is actually a strong incentive among those who participate on the private sector to give access to individuals so that they can improve their opportunities for profit, for information sharing. That's what's already been going on—it will continue. There is no need for the government to pretend that it needs to take leadership here. I think that's just political posturing."

<Moderator>
Senator McCain.

<Senator McCain>
"I believe that we do have a problem. And that is that there is a growing gap between the *haves* and *have-nots* in America, those that are able to take part in this information technology and those that haven't. We took a major step forward when we decided to wire every school and library in America to the Internet. That's a good program. We have to have step two, three, and four, which means good equipment, good teachers, and good classrooms. No, I wouldn't do it directly. But there's lots of ways that you can encourage corporations, who in their own self-interest, would want to provide . . . would receive tax benefits, would receive credit, and many other ways for being involved in the schools, in upgrading the quality of equipment that they have, the quality of the students, and thereby providing a much-needed well-trained workforce."

<Moderator>
Thank you. Mr. Forbes.

UNIT 14

態度や感情を表すイントネーション

声のトーンを上げ下げすることで、話し手はいろいろな態度や感情を表現することができます。少し大げさに聞こえるくらい感情を込めて発音する練習をしてみましょう。（感情を表す以外のイントネーションの働きについては Unit 15 を参照）

Exercise 14-1　　　　　　　　　　　　　　　　　　　　　　　　　　　　　CD 2-64

相づちなどの間投詞のイントネーションを見てみましょう。音声の後について繰り返してください。

1. uh-oh 　　　　　　（まずい！）
2. uh-huh 　　　　　　（相づち）
3. uh-uh 　　　　　　（ダメ）
4. uh-uh 　　　　　　（知らない）
5. hm 　　　　　　　（思案）
6. hm! 　　　　　　　（疑い、軽蔑、不満）
7. ah 　　　　　　　（なるほど）
8. aha! 　　　　　　（分かった！）

A. uh-huh 　　　　　（相づち）
B. uh-huh 　　　　　（なるほど）
C. uh-huh 　　　　　（本当に？）
D. uh-uh 　　　　　（ダメ）
E. uh-uh! 　　　　　（絶対ダメ）
F. uh-uh 　　　　　（それは違う）

Exercise 14-2　　　　　　　　　　　　　　　　　　　　　　　　　　　　　CD 2-65

I told you it wouldn't work! と I thought it would! をいろいろなイントネーションを使い読んでみます。音声の後について繰り返し発音してみましょう。

（怒り）　　　　　I told you it wouldn't work!　　I thought it would!
（興奮）　　　　　I told you it wouldn't work!　　I thought it would!

（不信、疑惑）	I told you it wouldn't work!	And I thought it would!
（自慢げ）	I told you it wouldn't work!	I thought it would!
（面白おかしい）	I told you it wouldn't work!	I thought it would!
（悲しみ）	I told you it wouldn't work!	I thought it would!
（安堵）	I told you it wouldn't work!	Whew! I thought it would!
（あきらめ）	I told you it wouldn't work!	I thought it would!

Exercise 14-3　　　　　　　　　　　　　　　　　　　　　　　CD 2-66

Really? と Maybe. をいろいろなイントネーションを使い発音してみましょう。音声の後について繰り返してください。

1.	Really?	（関心）	Maybe.	（一般的な可能性）
2.	Really?	（強い関心）	Maybe.	（思わせぶり）
3.	Really?	（退屈）	Maybe.	（退屈）
4.	Really?	（うれしいが信じられない）	Maybe.	（わずかな可能性）
5.	Really?	（嫌み）	Maybe.	（弁明）
6.	Really?	（悲しみ）	Maybe.	（悲しみ）
7.	Really?	（安堵）	Maybe.	（希望）
8.	Really?	（遠慮がちに質問）	Maybe.	（明言を避ける）
9.	Really?	（情報の確認）	Really.	（追認）

Exercise 14-4　　　　　　　　　　　　　　　　　　　　　　　CD 2-67

Who did it? と言われた人が I don't know. と返答する短い会話をいろいろなイントネーションを使い練習してみましょう。

1.	Who did it?	（関心）	I don't know.	（単に知らない）
2.	Who did it?	（尋問調）	I don't know.	（釈明）
3.	Who did it?	（怒り）	I don't know.	（強い主張）
4.	Who did it?	（何回も質問）	I don't know.	（強い否定）
5.	Who did it?	（嫌み）	I don't know.	（弁明）
6.	Who did it?	（悲しみ）	I don't know.	（絶望）
7.	Who did it?	（安堵）	I sure don't know.	（無関心）
8.	Who did it?	（遠慮がちに質問）	I don't know.	（陽気に）
9.	Who did it?	（迷惑）	I don't know.	（同じく迷惑）
10.	Who did it?	（うれしいが信じられない）	I don't know.	（知るわけがない）
11.	Who did it?	（驚き）	I don't know.	（不機嫌）

UNIT 15

最後に

最後に Alice put it on the shelf. という文を使って、英語のリズムとイントネーションが具体的にどのようにして生まれてくるのか見てみましょう。

まず、リズムの決定です。

① 各単語のストレスの位置を確認します。

      Alice put it on the shelf.

② 名詞、動詞、形容詞、副詞などの内容語のストレスはそのまま残りますが、それ以外の語は文中では弱くなりストレスが消えてしまいます。

      Alice put it on the **shelf.**

これで、文の基本的な強弱パターンができあがりました。

ここからはイントネーション（アクセントにより生み出される文全体のピッチの変化）の出番です。

③ メッセージを伝える上で重要な働きをする内容語（Alice, put, shelf）は他の語よりも目立たせる必要があるため、アクセントが置かれます。Unit 1 の最初でも見たように、アクセントを受ける単語のストレス音節ではピッチが大きく変化します。（以下では、' で示しています）

      '**Alice** '**put** it on the '**shelf.**

これで一応完成です。

④ ただ、ネイティブスピーカーはアクセントが3つあるときは、最初と最後のアクセントだけを残し、それ以外のアクセントを弱化させる傾向があります。（アクセントが弱化された音節は ° で示しています）

その結果、

　　　　ˈAlice ˚put it on the ˈshelf.

という発音が最も標準的な発音になります。Unit 1 で取り上げた Dogs eat bones. が **Dogs** eat **bones**. というアクセントパターンを取っていたのはこういう理由があるのです。アクセントが 4 個以上ある場合は、最初と最後以外は話し手の判断で比較的自由に弱化させることができます。

ちなみに、ˈAlice ˚put it on the ˈshelf. を発音するときは、Alice にアクセントを置いた後 the までは声の高さをあまり変えずに読み shelf で一気にピッチを下げるよう心がけてください（˚put はストレスが残っているため、it, on, the よりもはっきりと発音しますが、ここでピッチを大きく変えないよう注意しましょう）。

⑤　ここからは話し手の意図が絡んできます。英語では最後のアクセントは聞き手に一番注意を向けてほしい部分（＝強調したい部分）を示すと同時に（Unit 1 参照）、そこで重要情報が終わることも示しています。

　　1)　Alice put it on the ˈ**shelf**.
　　　　（アリスは、［テーブルではなく］**棚に置いた**）
　　2)　Alice ˈ**put** it on the shelf.
　　　　（アリスは、棚に［ぶつけたのではなく］**置いた**）
　　3)　ˈ**Alice** put it on the shelf.
　　　　（［キャシーではなく］**アリス**が棚に置いた）

1)〜3) はそれぞれ shelf, put, Alice が強調されている意味になりますが、同時に 2) は put まで、3) は Alice までが重要な情報で、これ以降は、極端な言い方をすれば聞こえなくてもそれほど差し障りのない情報だということも示しています。1) のように文の最後の名詞（内容語）に最後のアクセントが来る場合は、shelf を強調する意味にもなりますが、shelf まで、すなわち、文全体が重要情報（または新情報）であることを示している可能性もあり、前後の文脈がなければどちらの意味なのか判断できません。アクセントの位置を考えるときは、文中のどの情報に焦点を置きたいのかを考え、まず最後のアクセントの位置を決めましょう。その結果 3 カ所以上アクセントがある場合は、④のルールを適用してみるとよいでしょう。

もちろん、これらのルールはあくまで原則です。イントネーションの働きはこれ以外にもいろいろありますが、まずはここで紹介した使い方を頭に入れておいてください。

クラス用音声 CD 有り（非売品）

Sounds Like American [Text Only]
A Guide to Fluency in Spoken English

2010 年 1 月 20 日　初版発行
2023 年 2 月 20 日　Text Only 版第 1 刷

著　者　Ann Cook
編著者　三島 篤志
発行者　松村 達生
発行所　センゲージ ラーニング株式会社
　　　　〒 102-0073　東京都千代田区九段北 1-11-11　第 2 フナトビル 5 階
　　　　電話　03-3511-4392
　　　　FAX　03-3511-4391
　　　　e-mail: eltjapan@cengage.com
　　　　copyright © 2010 センゲージ ラーニング株式会社

装丁　　　　　㈱クリエーターズユニオン
組版　　　　　㈱興陽社
本文イラスト　イラストレーターズ モコ
印刷・製本　　㈱平河工業社

ISBN 978-4-86312-418-9